UNIX® Commands by Example

A Desktop Reference for Solaris®, UnixWare™, and SCO® UNIX®

David Elboth   Kent Dannehl P. C. Larsen

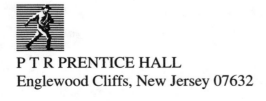

P T R PRENTICE HALL
Englewood Cliffs, New Jersey 07632

Cover design: *Jeannette Jacobs*
Acquisitions editor: *Mark L. Taub*
Manufacturing manager: *Alexis R. Heydt*

This book is derived from *UNIX: fra nybegynner til systemadministrator*,
first published in 1992 in Norwegian by Origo Forlag AS.

The publisher offers discounts on this book when ordered
in bulk quantities. From more information, contact:

> Corporate Sales Department
> PTR Prentice Hall
> 113 Sylvan Avenue
> Englewood Cliffs, NJ 07632
>
> Phone: 201-592-2863
> Fax: 201-592-2249

Printed in the United States of America
10 9 8 7 6 5 4 3 2 1

ISBN 0-13-103953-9

Prentice-Hall International (UK) Limited, *London*
Prentice-Hall of Australia Pty. Limited, *Sydney*
Prentice-Hall Canada Inc., *Toronto*
Prentice-Hall Hispanoamericana, S.A., *Mexico*
Prentice-Hall of India Private Limited, *New Delhi*
Prentice-Hall of Japan, Inc., *Tokyo*
Simon & Schuster Asia Pte. Ltd., *Singapore*
Editora Prentice-Hall do Brasil, Ltda., *Rio de Janeiro*

Contents

Contents

Contents

Introduction

This book is a reference to the most useful user-level UNIX® commands and concepts. It is aimed at beginning to intermediate-level UNIX users.

We do not attempt to provide information for every user-level command or concept found on UNIX systems, nor do we attempt to comprehensively describe all of the flags and options available for those commands we do discuss. Our conceptual articles cover only the most useful UNIX concepts. Our command articles focus on the most useful flags and options to the most useful UNIX commands.

Of course, UNIX manual pages are comprehensive. They present every command in detail. Unfortunately, they are also typically very dense and more often than not, incomprehensible. In addition, they suffer from one very acute shortcoming: they lack real-world, working examples.

We all know from our own experiences working with computers that we learn most effectively by example. Rather than read technical manuals, we scan them, looking for examples, then modify the examples to do what we need to get done.

This behavior was uppermost in our minds as we wrote this reference. Our primary goal was to simplify the understanding of UNIX commands by providing multiple examples for every command presented. This book contains over four-hundred examples of commands, flags, options, and environment variables. For example, our discussion of the **tar** command includes over thirty examples. And our discussion of **cpio** contains more than ten.

We have also included two long appendixes that contain detailed examples on using two of the UNIX system's most powerful features: shell programming and the **vi** editor. Again, this reflects our own experience that we learn most effectively by example.

In general, we assume that you know what command you are looking for. We have not attempted to group the commands by function, nor have we attempted to give the commands functional labels. We have seen both of these things done in other books, and we do not believe that they add value. Instead, we present the commands in alphabetical order. This greatly simplifies finding what you need. Each command article gives a quick overview of the command as well as the command syntax, function, and useful options and arguments to the command followed by working examples.

This approach to organizing our book does have drawbacks, at least for users brand new to UNIX. After all, we can understand how somebody familiar with

MS-DOS®may not think to look under **grep** for information on how to search the contents of a text file, or under **tar** for information on how to move files from a hard disk to a floppy disk. For these users, we have included a table at the back of the book (Appendix C) that maps some of the most common user-level tasks to the UNIX commands used to perform those tasks.

Our target platform is UNIX System V. However, due to the large number of System V implementations, we could not possibly do our development on every System V system. Instead, we have limited our development to the three most popular implementations of UNIX System V: Solaris® from Sun Microsystems, UnixWare™ from UNIX System Laboratories, Inc. and SCO® UNIX from The Santa Cruz Operation, Inc. Still, in the final analysis, System V implementations do not differ much on the user level, and so we believe that this book will be very useful to users of other System V implementations.

Notational Conventions

This book uses the following conventions.

- All examples are placed in shaded boxes.

- Filenames and directories are placed in italics, e.g., */u/lorim.*

- Commands and command options that are not filenames are placed in boldface type, e.g., **ls -a** */u/lynnsa.*

- Variables or places where the user must substitute actual text (place holders) are placed in bold-italic, e.g., **ls -a *directoryname*.**

- User input in a screen display or file and literal output that appears on the screen are placed in courier-bold, e.g., `This is how text appears that is displayed on the screen.`

- Items contained in square brackets ([...]) are optional.

- Key combinations mean hold down the first key while you press the second, e.g., **<Ctrl>b** means hold down the **<Ctrl>** key and press b.

Backing up a UNIX system

Backing up the system is important in a multiuser system. If the computer goes down, getting started again can become very expensive very quickly if you do not have a backup of your system's data.

The UNIX® system provides several ways of making backups. The easiest way is to use the system administration (sysadm) shells. These shells use different UNIX commands (for example, **restore, backup, cpio, tar** and **dd**) to perform system backup.

backup can make a full backup of a file system or only of those files being changed since the last backup. Similarly, **restore** either restores a complete file system or only a few files.

Both **tar** and **cpio** pack all the files into one large file. These two programs have options allowing you to perform selective backups based on (for example) date or filename. **cpio** can also work in connection with the **find** command making it much more flexible than **tar**. With **tar** and **cpio**, it is east to restore a single file.

dd is both a general converting tool and a backup program. With help of **dd**, you can quickly copy a complete file system from one hard disk to another. Similarly, if you wish to convert data from one system type to another (for example, EBCDIC to ASCII) **dd** is the tool.

NOTE:

Solaris systems also support the backup command **mt**. For more information on **mt**, see your Solaris system manuals.

See also:

backup; copy; cpio; cp; dd; find; restore; tar.

backup
backing up your data
(SCO UNIX and UnixWare)

With the **backup** command, you can back up either complete file systems or only those files changed since your last backup. **backup** can copy any data you specify either onto a floppy disk or tape depending on which option you choose.

NOTE:

Solaris systems only support the backup command **mt**. For more information on **mt**, see your Solaris system manuals.

If your **backup** requires more than 1 floppy or tape, you are prompted to insert another. **backup** always provides an estimate of how many floppies or tapes you will need to use.

In reality, backup is a shell script (or command file) using **find** and **cpio**. The format on the backup media is the same as the format used by **cpio**. **restore** is used to restore to disk data backed up with **backup**.

When you are using **backup**, the floppies have to be formatted before use. Unless you use mini-cartridge tapes, it is not necessary to format tapes.

Command:
backup [-f *files* | -u *"user1..."* | -c | -p | -d *device* | -t]
or
backup -h

Function:
Backs up complete file system or single directories or files.

Options:

-h   Gives a historical record of previous backups. A useful option telling you when the last backup was made and whether it was partial or complete.

-f *files* Makes backups of the files specified. Filenames may contain wildcards.

-u *user1* Makes a backup of a user's home directory. At a minimum one user must be specified, but there is no upper limit. To specify more than one user, use double quotation marks, for example: "Peter Philip" .

-c   Specifies a complete backup. All files changed since the system was installed are backed up. If you have completed an incremental or partial backup since system installation, all files modified since that time are backed up. Otherwise, all files modified since the last complete backup are backed up.

-p   Specifies a partial backup. Backs up only those files modified since the last backup. Before you can use of **-p** , however, you must have made a full backup.

-d *device* Specifies which backup device to use (*/dev/rfd0 /dev/rct0*--SCO, */dev/rmt/ctape1*--UnixWare™, etc.).

-t   Specifies that the device is a tape. This option must be used if the device specified with the **-d** option is a tape.

Examples (SCO® UNIX and UnixWare):

backup -u david -d */dev/rdsk/f03ht*
Makes a floppy backup copy of user david's home directory.

backup -u "peter ann greg kentd" -d */dev/rmt/ctape1*
Makes a tape backup of the home directories of the users peter, ann, greg and kentd.

---

backup -t -c
Makes a complete tape backup of all files changed since the system was installed.

backup -h
Produces a historical record of earlier backups.

See also:
copy; cpio; cp; dd; restore; tar.

Bourne shell
Configuring your work environment

If you use the Bourne shell (defined by the system administrator when your account is created), you use the file, *.profile* to define your initial login environment. *.profile* configures each login session you start. The *.profile* file is executed each time you log onto your system.

This file usually specifies things like terminal type, mail box and command search path, etc. Your default umask can also be set up here. (For more about the umask, see **umask** later in this book). Note that unlike C-shell and Korn shell, the Bourne shell does not support aliasing. For more information on aliasing, see the articles on C-shell and Korn shell below.

If you use the Bourne shell, you can logout by entering <Ctrl-d> or **exit** at any prompt.

Options and environment variables

The following are important Bourne shell environment variables and options. Note that variables are all uppercase. Environment variables are always written with capital letters and define a given user's environment.

PATH	Command search path.
CDPATH	Search path for the **cd** command.
LOGNAME	Your user name.
TERM	Terminal type, e.g., ansi.
HOME	Users home directory.
MAIL	Type of mailer used for electronic mail.
MAILCHECK	How often (in seconds) mail is checked.
PS1	Primary prompt.
PS2	Secondary prompt.
IFS	Internal field separator.

If you do not specify values, the Bourne shell assigns defaults for the environment variables **PATH, PS1, PS2** and **IFS. HOME** is always set when you login to the system. For environment variables to be activated, they must be defined and then exported. Environment variables are always written with capital letters and, once defined and exported, are part of your user operating environment. Once defined and exported, all environment variables are inherited by future shells. Note that after defining an environment variable, you must always export it. Also note the example of a user's *.profile* at the end of this article.

PATH   Controls where the shell looks for commands to be executed. Once defined, **PATH** defines part of the search path for the shell interpreter. Without the **PATH** command, you can only run programs and commands found in your local directory. If you receive the error message "Command not found", it may mean that the shell did not find the program in any of the directories specified by **PATH**. While you can set **PATH** from any command line, it is usually set up in a user's *.profile* and looks something like this:

```
PATH=/bin:/usr/bin:$HOME/bin:
export PATH
```

CDPATH   Specifies the search path for the cd command. Once this path is set the shell interpreter uses the directories named in CDPATH as working directories for the cd command.

TERM   Specifies the terminal type. Required by some commands (e.g., vi) that use the entire screen for output. To set a fixed terminal type in your *.profile*, include a line resembling the following:

```
TERM=vt100
```

HOME   Every user's home directory is defined as an environment variable called HOME. Thus, for example, you can use HOME to help define your PATH environment variable.

MAIL   Has no default value. It must be set either by the user or by the system administrator. The name of the user's electronic mailbox is usually placed in */usr/spool/mail*. MAIL defines or changes the path and filename of the mailbox. For example, you might have a line like the following in your *.profile*:

```
MAIL=/usr/spool/mail/`logname`
```

This definition tells the system to deliver your mail to a file in */usr/bin/mail* named after a user's login. For MAIL environment variables to be activated, you must first define them and then export them (see examples below).

MAILCHECK Specifies how often (in seconds) your mailbox is checked. For example:

`MAILCHECK=360`

specifies that your mail file will be checked every 6. minutes. The default value of MAILCHECK is 10 minutes (600 seconds). If you set MAILCHECK=0, the mail system checks each time you receive a new prompt (i.e., each time you press <Enter>).

PS1   Defines your prompt. The default value for the prompt in a Bourne shell, is the $ character. You can change this default value in your *.profile*. For example the line:

`PS1=Give command:`

defines the prompt to be the text "Give command".

PS2   Defines a secondary prompt. You see this prompt when your shell expects more input. By default, PS2 is set to >. For example,

`PS2=+`

defines the secondary prompt to be the character, "+"(plus).

IFS   IFS defines the variable used as field separator. Internal field separators usually are space, tab and new line. For example,

`IFS=,`

defines the , (comma) as the field separator.

Example of a *.profile* **file:**

```
:
#
# User $HOME/.profile - commands executed at login time
#
PATH=/bin:/usr/bin:$HOME/bin:.
MAIL=/usr/spool/mail/`logname`
umask 022
eval `tset -m ansi:ansi -m :\?ansi -r -s -Q`
export PATH MAIL
```

With this *.profile*, the system prompts you for the terminal type if none is defined for your terminal device (e.g., *tty01*, *tty1a*, *pts000*). The default terminal type is *ansi*. If you login with the above *.profile*, you will see a line resembling the following:

```
TERM = (ansi)
```

If you press <Enter> at this prompt, you define the terminal type as *ansi*. If you wanted a type other than *ansi* (e.g., vt100) , you would enter **vt100** at the prompt and then press <Enter>.

See also:

App. A-about shell scripts; C-shell; Korn shell; umask.

cal
print a calendar

The **cal** command displays the calendar for the present month and year.

Command:
cal [*month*] [*year*]

Function:
Displays a calendar.

Options:
No options.

Examples:

cal
Displays the calendar for the previous, present and next month of the present year.

cal 4 1994
Displays the following :

```
     April 1994
 S   M Tu  W Th  F   S
                 1   2
 3   4  5  6  7  8   9
10  11 12 13 14 15  16
17  18 19 20 21 22  23
24  25 26 27 28 29  30
```

---

calendar
receiving messages from your calendar file

    calendar reminds you of activities that you have scheduled. When you execute the command, the program searches for a file named *calendar* in your home directory. If the file is found, **calendar** mails you any lines that contain today's or tomorrow's date. The *calendar* file is a text file that contains dates to remember.

Command:
    calendar

Function:
    Checks the file *calendar* in your home directory to see if you have any appointments. If you have an appointment, **calendar** mails you the information entered for that date.

Options:
    Because of the variation between systems, see your UNIX reference handbook or use **man calendar** for option information.

Example:

    For **calendar** to work, you must create the *calendar* file yourself. It must be called *calendar* and it must be readable by everybody.

    Each single line in the file, *calendar* must include a date. The program is flexible concerning where to place the date, as long as the month is placed prior to the date, for example, May 3. If you write * instead of the month, for example, * 24, calendar sends you a reminder on the 24th of each month. The month may be abbreviated, but it must be unique. For example, in your *calendar* file all of the following are acceptable::

```
aug 7
august 7
8/7
```


Creating your personal calendar

To create your own personal calendar, complete the following steps:

1.. Use an ASCII editor (such as **vi**), or the **cat** command to create a personal *calendar* file in your *$HOME* directory.

2. If you use **cat** enter the following::
   cat > *calendar*

3. Enter your calendar items. For example,

```
jun 14                          Appointment with Prentice Hall
jul 29                          I am 40 years today
Oct 6                           Meeting with the President
March 8th of the year 1994      Mother is 70 years old
Important Sep 7                 Dinner with Peter at 7.00 pm
Sep 9                           Off work
```

4. Enter <Ctrl d>

5. To be able to receive messages on any given day., the **calendar** program must be run when you log into the computer that day. This may be done in one of three ways:

   - Manually type **calendar** from the prompt each time you log into the system.

   - Start **calendar** automatically each time you log in. For example, this may be set up in your *.profile* (if you use the Bourne or Korn shell) or in your *.login* or *.cshrc* (if you use C-shell). In either case, the **calendar** command should be the last command in the file.

   - Schedule the calendar program to run as a fixed task (**cron** job) in the background in */usr/spool/cron/crontabs/adm* (SCO) or */usr/spool/cron/crontabs/root* (UnixWare and Solaris).

If you set up calendar to run as a fixed task for all users, you must set file permissions so that each user's *calendar* file can be read by everyone. For moreinformation on setting permissions see **chmod**. For more information on scheduling commands to be executed at intervals, see your **crontab** manual page. Your calendar file items are sent to you as electronic mail.

Files:
/usr/lib/calprog (calculates today's and tomorrow's date); */etc/passwd; /tmp/cal**.

See also:
Bourne shell; C-shell; Korn shell; mail.

cancel
cancel a print job

Cancels print requests made with **lp** or **lpr**.

Command:
cancel [*argument*]

Function:
Removes a print-job from the print queue.

Options:
No options.

Arguments:
Either the printer name or print job number(s). The print job number is a text string consisting of the name of the printer and a job number. Immediately after execution of the **lpr** or the **lp** command, the number of the print-job is displayed on the screen. You may also use the **lpstat**-command to find the job-number.

Examples:

The command:
cancel printer-233
cancels the print job "printer-233".

To cancel 2 jobs at the same time, enter:
cancel laser-22 laser-24
Cancels print jobs laser-22 and laser-24.

Files:
/etc/lp/*; /var/spool/lp/* ; /usr/spool/lp/* (SCO).

See also:
lp; lpstat; print spooling.

cat
write files to the screen

With **cat**, you can display your text files on the screen. **cat** means concatenate, and was designed to help users combine several files into one file. Note that if you use **cat** without options or arguments, **cat** expects data from the standard input channel, i.e., the keyboard.

Command:
    cat [-s] [-v] [*filename[s]* ...]

Function:
Displays the content of a text file on the screen, allows the user to concatenate files or echoes text from the standard input (usually the keyboard) on the screen .

Options:
-s   No messages are given about non-existent files.

-v   Shows control characters, for example ^X, ^?.

Arguments:
The **cat** command can take any *filename* (or series of *filenames*) as an argument. **cat** echoes the contents of *filename* to the screen. Without arguments, **cat** echoes input from the keyboard to the screen.

Examples:

The following is an example **cat** with no options or arguments:
cat

```
This is an example of text written with the help of
This is an example of text written with the help of
the command cat.
the command cat.
```

```
Terminate cat by entering control d.
Terminate cat by entering control d.
```
<Ctrl d>

Each line is repeated. The first line is displayed as you write. When you press
<Enter> **cat** echoes displays your text on the screen.

The following line:
cat -v *davidtext*
displays the text file, *davidtext* with all its control characters.

The command:
cat *letter1 answer*
displays both the files *letter1* and *answer* on the screen.

The command:
cat *letter1 answer >newletter*
combines (concatenates) *letter1* and *answer* into the new file, *newletter*.

See also:
cp.

cd
change directory

cd (change directory) changes your working directory. You use **cd** to change from one directory to another. For example, if you are working in the directory, */u/maryst/word* and you want to work on files in the directory, */u/laura/games*, you issue the command:

    cd */u/laura/games*

Command:
    cd [*directoryname*]

Function:
    Change the working directory.

Argument:
    directoryname   Path name of the directory you want to work in.

If you enter cd without any arguments, you are brought automatically to your *$HOME* directory, (for example, */home/david* or */usr/david*).

Examples:

If you are not using the restricted shell, **cd** (change directory) changes the current working directory to any directory specified in the argument. For example,

cd */etc* Moves to the directory *etc*.
cd *..*   Moves one directory (node) upwards.
cd *../../* Moves two directories (nodes) upwards.
cd */*   Moves to the top level (*root*) wherever you may be.
cd *../dev* Moves one node upward and thereafter downward to the
         directory *dev*.

Other examples of the **cd** command are:

cd /
Moves up to the root directory, i.e., to the top level of the tree structure. After
changing directories, use **pwd** (print working directory) to confirm that you really
are in the *root* directory. **ls -la** lists the files in the root directory.

cd ../david
Moves a step further upwards and then down to david.

cd ../../etc
Moves two steps up and then down to */etc*. It would have been easier to enter
cd /etc

cd /home/david/wp/files
Moves directly to the directory, *files*.

If you are working in */usr/david*, the command:
cd uniplex
changes to the directory */usr/david/uniplex*. The alternative is to enter the full path
name
cd /usr/david/uniplex

To move from */usr/david/uniplex/txt* to the neighbor directory *data*, enter
cd ../data

To move two directory levels up to */usr/david*, enter
cd ../../

If you are the user, david, you may enter **cd** without any arguments. No matter
where you are in the directory tree, this always brings you to your home directory
(*$HOME*).

See also:
Directories; Files; mkdir; pwd; rmdir.

UNIX commands by example

chgrp
changing group identity

The owner of a file or directory can change its group identification (ID). If group access to a file is restricted, only those who are group members have access to that file.

Command:
chgrp [*group*] [*argument*] ...

Function:
Changes the group ID of file(s) and/or directory(ies).

Argument:
File(s) and/or directory(ies)

group may either be group name or group number. In most cases, only the owner or the system administrator may change a file or directory group.

Examples:

chgrp technical *
Changes the group ID for all the files in the working directory, to "technical".

chgrp technical .*
Changes the group ID for all the system (".") files.

chgrp Support *
Changes the group ID for all the files in the working directory to Support.

chgrp Support .*
Again, changes the system files.

chgrp 50 text file
Changes the group ID of all the files in the working directory to 50. The file
/etc/group contains a complete list of groups and group numbers.

See also:

chown; chmod; newgrp.

UNIX commands by example

chmod
changing file access permission

Because UNIX is a multiuser, multitasking operating system, setting file access is very important. The command for changing file access codes is **chmod**. With this command, you can change the different access codes for files, or directories. As a rule, only the owner of the file and the system administrator can change the access codes. Default access permission is determined by the **umask** setting.

Command:
Symbolic syntax:
chmod [*who*] + - = [*permissions* ...] *file/directory* ...

Octal syntax:
chmod [*access permission*] [*argument*]

Function:
Changes the rights to read, write and execute file(s) and directory(ies). Also changes several specialized access codes (s, t, S, etc.).

access permission or mode determines who has access rights to a given file or directory. **chmod** allows you to change access permissions on files and directories These access codes or modes may be changed using either symbolic (letters and Boolean operators) or octal (numeric) code.

Changing permissions using symbolic syntax
who refers to the recipient of the revised access permission. Note that unless you are *root*, you cannot alter permissions on files that you do not own. Valid arguments are:

u	Designates the user/file owner. This argument means that you are going to alter permissions for yourself.
g	Designates users with the same group ID as the user/file owner. This argument indicates that you want to alter the privileges that group members have in relation to a file.

o   Designate all other users. This argument indicates that you intend to alter what all other users (those other than yourself who are not group members) can do with the file.

a   Designates all users (default). This argument indicates that you intend to alter what all users can do with the file.

a is the default. That is, if you do not specify whose access you want to change, the **chmod** command is valid for all.

To change access rights, use the following operators:

+   adds right

-   removes right

=   rather than add or subtract from existing permissions, = sets the permissions to whatever access rights you designate.

permissions are as follows:

r   (read). Permission to read or view a file (or directory) but not to alter it.

w   (write). Permission to write to the file. Anyone with write permission can alter a file.

x   (execute or run): Anyone with execute permission on an executable file can execute it.

Specialized access codes are as follows:

S   Undefined bit state (Only Solaris and UnixWare)

s   If a file is executable, sets the file permission to the ID of the person or group executing it--when it is executed. **chmod u+s** sets the user name for the file, and **chmod g+s** sets the group for the file. All other combinations have no effect.

t   Sets sticky bit on a directory. When the sticky bit is set on a directory, no file in that directory can be removed except by the owner or *root*.

| T | Undefined bit state (Only Solaris and UnixWare). |
| l | File lock. When set, only one user at a time may access the file. |

Changing permissions using octal syntax

As an alternative to changing permissions with **r**, **w**, **x**, you can use a 3-digit octal number. The numbers correspond to access permissions. They are listed in the following table:

Octal Code	Permissions	Maps to
7	read, write and execute	rwx
6	read and write	rw-
5	read and execute	r-x
4	read	r--
3	write and execute	-wx
2	write	-w-
1	execute	--x
0	none	---

Note that octal syntax is absolute. When you change file permissions with octal, what you designate with **chmod** is what you get. If you use **chmod** symbolically to change permissions, your commands are relative to the file permissions already present. Thus **chmod u+x** *filename* adds user execute permission to what is already there. If you issued the command **chmod 100** *filename*, the file has only user execute permissions. When using octal syntax to change access permissions, the first digit specifies the owner, the second specifies the group, and the third digit specifies access for other users.

Examples:

Octal syntax:

chmod 444 *facefile*
Allows read permission to everyone for the file, *facefile*.

chmod 777 *not.important*
Allows all users read, write, and execute permission for the file *not.important*.

chmod 644 *facefile*
Allow the file owner read and write permission, and allows everybody else read permission for the file, *facefile*.

chmod 755 *not.important*
Allows the owner read, write, and execute permissions and allows everybody else read and execute permission for the file *not.important*.

Symbolic syntax:

chmod u+x *program*
Gives the user him- or herself permission to execute *program*.

chmod o+xw *program*
Allows all other users permission to execute and write to the file *program*.

chmod a+rwx *batch*
Allows everybody permission to read, write and execute the file *batch*.

chmod g-r *letter*
Denies everybody in a user's group permission to read the file *letter*.

chmod ug=rwx *report*
Allows the user and everyone in his or her group to read, write and execute the file *report*.

chmod g+r, o+r *text*
Allows everyone in the group as well as all others to read the file *text*.

chmod +x *not.important*
Gives all the users execute permission on the file *not.important*. Note that if the file is not a program or a script of some type, it will not do anything.

chmod a-x *letter*
Removes execute permission for everyone.

chmod +l *datafile*
Locks *datafile* for all users immediately after the file is opened or executed.

chmod =rwx,g+s *testfile*
Allows everyone to read, write, and execute the file. Also when any user executes or opens the file, sets the group ID to that of the person who opens or executes the file.

chmod u+t *calc*
Places a sticky bit on the directory *calc*. Now only the owner and system administrator (*root*) can remove files from that directory.

See also:
chgrp; chown; Files; newgrp.

chown
changing file owner

With **chown**, you can change the owner of file(s) and directory(ies). When you change the owner of a file or a directory, the file or directory is not physically moved. Note that once you give a file to another user, the file is theirs and you cannot get it back without their help.

Command:
chown [*owner*] [*files*]

Function:
Changes the owner of a file or directory.

Arguments:

owner   May be a user name or a user number. Normally only the owner or the system administrator may change file or directory owners.

files   Name of file(s) given new owner.

Examples:

chown eric *
eric becomes the owner of all files (except system files e.g., *.profile*) in the present directory.

chown david */usr/david/**
david becomes the owner of all files in the directory */usr/david.*

chown 155 *annes.fil*
The user with ID number 155 becomes the owner of *annes.file*

                UNIX commands by example

Files:
/etc/passwd; /etc/group.

See also;
chgrp; Files; newgrp.

Commands, options and arguments

You give commands to UNIX via the shell. For example, if you want to display the content of a directory, you do the following:

1.   Type **ls** (the command displaying the contents of a directory)
2.   Press <Enter> to give the signal to UNIX to execute the command.
3.   The shell displays the directory's content on the screen. For example, ls produces the following on this machine:

```
batch
c-files
dhry.c
doc
mbox
english.inn
text
usr
```

Command syntax

Most commands have different versions and options. The version you use depends on which options you need. In this book, when we want to demonstrate the syntax of a command with its options and/or arguments, we use the following convention:

Command:

ls [*option*] [*argument*]

The command is the name of the program or the function to be executed. The command is always specified first. Normally, there is a space between commands, options and arguments.

If there are options, it means that you have more than one way to specify how the (main) command is going to be executed. Depending on your own choice and need, you may choose either to specify or not to specify any given option. Normally, the first option must be prefixed by a - (hyphen).

UNIX commands by example

An argument provides more specific information about how the command should work. If the word argument is specified inside square brackets (e.g., *[argument]*), it is up to the user to supply the argument as a type of additional message.

To show the difference between commands, options and arguments we have used the following conventions:

Examples:

bold	Commands, options and arguments.
italics	Filenames.
bold italics	Place holders for information that must be supplied by the user (usually an argument to a command).
`courier`	Screen output or input that a user must enter verbatim in a file.

Below is an example of a command with one option:

l -a

l is one of the commands that display a directory contents to the screen. The **-a** option signals to UNIX that you want to display the entire contents of a directory, including system files (those files preceded by a "."). The above command produces the following:

```
total 20
drwx------    6 david      Writer          928    Dec 26 19:56 .
drwxrwxr-x   27 root       auth            432    Nov 18 18:02 ..
-rw-------    1 david      Writer          771    Jun 08 1991 .cshrc
-rw-------    1 david      Writer          554    Jun 08 1991 .login
drwxr-xr-x    2 david      Writer         1184    Dec 24 11:45 batch
drwxr-xr-x    5 david      Writer          192    Jun 26 1991  c-fil
drwxr-xr-x    2 david      Writer           48    Dec 26 19:56 data
-rw-r--r--    1 david      Writer          405    Dec 26 19:55 fil
drwxr-xr-x    3 david      Writer           48    Jun 09 1991 usr
```

A command may also be written without any options and arguments. In that case, the command is executed in its default way. This means that the command has a standard option and/or a standard argument used when no other options and arguments are specified. Again, let us use the command **ls** as an example.

ls
Without any options or arguments, this command displays the directory content of your working directory. If the **ls** command were run on the same directory as the **l -a** command above, the output would resemble the following:

```
batch
c-fil
data
fil
usr
```

Pipes, filters and redirection

UNIX allows you to connect commands in several ways. For example,

ls | wc -l

ls displays the contents of the working directory. **wc -l** counts the number of lines in the display. These types of connections between commands are called pipes. Pipes allow you to use the result of the first command as input for the second. "|" is the symbol for a pipe.

A pipe functions as a kind of a filter. Each program in the sequence performs certain operations with the data. Each program, that is, filters the data before sending them further on to the next program. Programs that perform operations on data before "piping" them on are often called filters.

In the example above (**ls | wc -l**), a keyboard command causes UNIX to fetch information from the directory and display it on the screen. As we have seen, it is also possible to take that information and "pipe" it somewhere else. For example, the command

ls > *filename*

redirects the output from the command **ls** into the file, *filename*. The standard input channel (data-in) for **ls** is the keyboard, and the standard output channel (data-out) is the screen. That is, in the example we redirect the standard output from the screen to a file.

We can do other things with the standard output as well. For example, the command

ls > /dev/lp0

outputs the directory content to the printer instead of to the screen. Both of these commands are said to "redirect" the standard output.

See also:

Pipes and filters; Redirection; Standard input, output and error.

copy
copying whole directories

The **copy** command copies directories. With **copy** you can copy complete file systems, since this command automatically generates directories while copying. This command is only supported on SCO UNIX and UnixWare platforms.

Command:
  copy [-**anmrvo**] [*source-directory*] [*destination-directory*]

Function:
  Copies files and directories.

Options:

-a	Prompts the user before starting.
-n	Requires the destination file to be new.
-m	Retains the original date and time of the source file in the destination file.
-r	Includes all subdirectories.
-v	Shows all messages while copying.
-o	Copies each file, keeping the original owner and group.

Arguments:

source directory	The directory to be copied from.
destination directory	The directory to be copied to

Examples:

copy . */tmp/security*
In this example, all the files in the current working directory are copied to the subdirectory */tmp/security*.

copy -vr * */tmp/data*
All the files in the directory (and the subdirectories) where the command is executed, are copied to the directory */tmp/data*. Since we specified the **-v** option, we can see the files on the screen as they are copied.

copy */usr/chess/match /usr/game/dart /usr/fun*
All the files in the directory */usr/chess/match* and */usr/game/dart* are copied to the directory */usr/fun*. Subdirectories are not included in this operation.

copy -vrom */etc/conf /kernel*
A full copy of */etc/conf* (with subdirectories) is places under the directory */kernel*. Each file copied retains the original owner name and group name. The original date and time in the source file will be kept by the destination file.

See also:
cp; cpio; ln; mv; rm.

cp
copy files

With **cp** you can copy single files or groups of files. At a minimum, to use **cp,** you must have read access to the file and write access to the destination directory.

Command:
cp *file1 file2*
or
cp *files directory*

Function:
Copies one or several files to a new filename or directory.

Options:
Because **cp** options vary so much among products, see your UNIX reference handbook or enter **man cp** at a UNIX prompt for more information on supported options.

Arguments:
file1	Name of the file to be copied (the source).
file2	Name of the new file (destination).
directory	Name of the destination directory.

Examples:

cp *report report1*
Copies *report* to a new file called *report1*.

cp **nrf text/*
Copies all files ending with nrf to the subdirectory *text/*. The new files keep their original filenames, user-IDs, group-IDs, etc.

UNIX commands by example

cp *letter1* **letter2** */usr/letterdir*
Copies the files *letter1* and *letter2* to the directory */usr/letterdir*

See also:
copy; cpio; ln; mv; rm; chmod.

cpio
backing up data with cpio

cpio is as old as **tar**, but it is not used as frequently because of its arcane syntax. However, it is an excellent tool for data transfer. Both **backup** and **restore** use cpio. With the help of **cpio** and **find,** you can make backups of any type of data on a UNIX-system.

Command:
cpio -o [Bvc] [*destination file or device*]
or
cpio -i [Bcdmvtu] [*file* ...]
or
cpio -p [dmvu] [*directory*]

Note that **cpio** usually receives its list of files to be copied or archived from some other command via a pipe (see "Commands, options and arguments"). Thus, **cpio** commands usually have a syntax similar to the following:
find */usr/game* **-name** *chess.* * **-print** I **cpio -ocv** */dev/rct0*
where **find** produces a list of absolute file names that are piped to **cpio. cpio,** in turn, archives the files on */dev/rct0*--a tape drive.

Function:

cpio -o	(copy out). Given a list of files piped to it from another command (for example **ls** or **find**), **cpio -o** copies files from their original location to a tape or floppy backup device; or to a cpio format file.
cpio -i	(copy in). Restores files archived with **cpio -o** from tape, floppy disk, or file.
cpio -p	(pass) Similar to **cpio -o** but instead of copying files to a tape, floppy or **cpio** file, **cpio -p** copies the list of files piped to it to a different directory or filesystem.

Options:

-B	Sets block size for input and output to 5120 bytes per record. The default buffer size is device dependent unless you use this option or the **-C** option.
-c	Places header information in ASCII format for increased portability. Use this option when the source computer and the destination computer use different UNIX types.
-C *bufsize*	I/O Blocks are set to *bufsize* bytes and sent to a character-special device (e.g., tape archive). The default buffer size is device dependent unless you use this option or the **-B** option.
-d	Makes directories when necessary.
-m	Retains original file modification times. If you do not want to retain original file modification times, do **not** use this option.
-t	Displays a table of contents of a **cpio** archive. If the option is used, no files are copied.
-v	(verbose). Use this option if you want to observe the names of the files being copied.

Arguments:

file arguments can make use of wildcards. The *file* argument is used when using **cpio -i** to restore from floppy or tape. If no *file* argument is specified, all files are included.

NOTE:

The following examples use device driver names for floppy and tape drives. These device driver names are not used on all systems. For more information on how devices are named on your system, look at the device names in */etc/default/tar* or see "**tar**" below.

cpio

Examples:

ls | cpio -o >>/dev/fd0
Copies all files in your current directory to floppy disk.

ls /usr/david**| cpio -o >>**/dev/rct0
Copies all files in the directory /usr/david to tape.

ls | cpio -oc > class
Copies all files in your current directory to the file class. The -c option ensures portability to different types of UNIX systems.

cpio -i < class
Restores all the files from the file class.

cpio -iBdm /etc/termcap **<** /dev/rmt/0a
Restores /etc/termcap from tape.

cpio -itvc </dev/rfd048ds9
Restores all files on the floppy disk.

cpio -i </dev/fd0 wpterm
Restores wpterm from floppy disk.

cpio -i < /dev/rct0 *
Restores all files on the tape.

cpio -itv </dev/rmt/ctape1
Displays the content of the tape to screen.

Instead of using **ls,** you can use pipes with **find, echo** or **cat** to create a file list which is then piped to **cpio**.

find . -print | cpio -o > /dev/rdsk/f05ht
Copies the content of the current working directory and all of its subdirectories to a floppy disk.

find / -depth -print | cpio -odv > */dev/rct0*
Backs up the entire disk to tape. To restore, enter:

cpio -idmv */* < */dev/rct0*

See also:
backing up UNIX systems; copy; cp; cpio; dd; restore; tar.

csh
invoking the C–shell command interpreter

csh is a command interpreter. It (like the Bourne and Korn shells) helps the user to control the operating system kernel. Unlike the Bourne shell, **csh** is a more flexible interactive command interpreter. Unlike Korn shell **csh** uses a syntax based in the C programming language. If your login shell is C-shell your **csh** UNIX session begins by executing commands in your *.login* and *.cshrc* files. Typing **csh** at any UNIX command line automatically starts a C-shell (a subshell).

See also:
Bourne shell; C-shell; Korn shell.

C-shell
Configuring your work environment

If you use C-shell (defined when your account is created), you use the file , *.login* ,to define your initial login environment. *.login* configures each login session you start. After logging in, your shell environment is further defined in your *.cshrc* (C-shell define) file. *.cshrc* is read every time you start a new shell. You can use either file to configure important parts of your C-shell environment.

You exit the C shell by entering **exit** or **logout** at the system prompt.

Shell commands, options and environment variables

set	Sets variables.
unset	Removes variables.
alias	Makes an alias for a command or group of commands.
unalias	Removes an alias.
history	Maintains the list of remembered commands.
pwd	Prints working directory (same in C- and Bourne shell).
ignoreof	Ignores end of file (eof). Prevents shell exit with **<Ctrl-d>**.
noclobber	Prevents overwriting of files while redirecting.
home	Name of the home directory.
prompt	Gives or sets the command prompt.
repeat	Repeats command.
path	Sets path.
rehash	Builds new hash table.
source *file*	Cause the shell to read information in *file*. **source** can be used to reread your *.login* and *.cshrc* after updates, without requiring you to logout.

Usually there are system wide defaults for the most common C-shell commands, options and variables. To change or add to the defaults, you must enter the commands yourself. Once they are defined, they become part of your user operating environment. Once environment variables are defined, they are inherited by future shells. C-shell variables can be set on the command line or in your *.login* or *.cshrc* files. If you define them in your *.login* or *.cshrc* files, they are set every time you log on or start a new C-shell. If you define them on a C-shell command line, they belong to the defining shell and to any shell started by that shell. In addition to examples of the most common C-shell commands, sample *.login* and *.cshrc* files are supplied at the end of this article.

set   Use **set** to set C-shell environment variables. You use shell variables to control the shell's behaviour. Several variables configure C-shell behaviour. Some of the more important ones are listed here.

The syntax is

set *variable=value*

For example, to set the number of commands that the C-shell will remember to 20, issue the command

set history=20

Certain variables have a predefined meaning for C-shell. To use them you simply set the variable. For example,

set noclobber

Once a variable value is set, to use it you must prefix the variable name with a $ (for example *$HOME*). The variable name must always start with a character letter and on most systems is limited to 20 characters. To see a list of the C-shell variables that have already been set, enter the command **set** without any arguments.

unset   Use **unset** to remove a variable. The syntax is

unset *variablename*

For example, if you issue the command

unset path

at the C-shell prompt, you remove the existing command path definition.

alias Use **alias** to give new or different names to commands or combinations of commands. To set the aliases permanently, you can set them up in your *.cshrc* file. If you do, each time you start a C-shell, your alias definitions are included. The syntax is

alias *name definition*

For example, the following command "aliases" the command **l** for the command **ls -la**

alias l ls -la

To include arguments in an alias, use the character combination \!*. If you do use \!*, you must use single quotations ('). For example,

alias print 'pr -n \!:* | lp'

and

alias termscreen 'setenv TERM qvt119w;tset -r'

As with **set**, if no arguments are used with the alias command, all aliases set for the shell are displayed.

unalias Use **unalias** to undo an alias. The syntax is

unalias *aliasname*

For example,

unalias print and
unalias termscreen

would unset the aliases we set above.

history Use **history** to instruct the C-shell to remember as many commands as you specify. In most cases, we define a value between 10 and 25 commands. The syntax is

history=*n*

where *n* is the number of commands to be recorded
(remembered). For example,

set history=20

sets the number of remembered commands to 20--an excellent
number as it corresponds to the number that can be displayed on
one screen.

Once C-shell remembers a command, that command can be re-
ferred to if you want to reuse it or any part of it. After setting the
history variable, to see your command "history", enter **history**
without any arguments. To refer to a previous command simply
prefix your reference with a "bang", i.e., with an exclamation
mark. For example,

!-3	Restarts the third command from the end.
!!	Restarts the last command.
!test	Restarts the last command having the string test included.
!56:s/Take/Got	Finds command line 56 and substitutes the text string Got for Take, and then reexecutes the command.
^bin^usr	Takes the last command and interchanges bin with usr, and then executes the command again.

All command lines and arguments on a given line are numbered.
Thus, to refer to a command and argument, make use of
!commandnumber to give the command and a
:argumentnumber to give the argument number. The command
name is argument number 0, first argument is number 1, the next
number 2, etc. You can always refer to the last argument by $ and

to the first by the symbol ^ (hat). If all the arguments are going to be used, specify *. You can also use the history commands in connection with other UNIX commands.

pwd   Use to print your current working directory. For example,

pwd
`/usr/laurad`

noclobber   Use to prevent C-shell from overwriting an existing file. For example, if the file *letter1* already exists, the command:

ls -la > *letter1*

returns the message

`letter1: File exists.`

home   Use to set a user's home directory. For example, the command

set home = */u/laura*

set the user's home directory to */u/laura*.

rehash   Instructs C-shell to recompile its database containing command locations. If you place new executable programs in any directory already in the your search path, C-shell cannot find them unless you run **rehash**. Running **rehash** causes C-shell to search through the command path to create a database for executable programs. This database (or hash table) enables your shell to find and execute programs in your path.

ignoreeof   Prevents C-shell from exiting (ending the session) when it receives an end-of-file (eof) command from a terminal.

prompt   Use to define the C-shell command prompt. For example, the command

set prompt="` `` `pwd` `` **`>"**
alias cd 'setenv CWD `pwd`; chdir \!:*; set prompt="` `` `pwd` `` **`>'"**

sets the C-shell prompt to be the current working directory.

repeat   Use to repeat a command several times. The syntax is

repeat *number command*

where ***number*** is the number of times you want to repeat the command and ***command*** is the command you want repeated. For example,

repeat 2 history

repeats the history command twice.

path   The shell variable path controls which directories your C-shell session will check for executable commands and programs. If an executable command or program is not in your current path, C-shell cannot find and execute it. Usually, your system administrator will set a default path, but any commands you need that are not in the default path must be added manually.

If you spelled the command correctly and you see the error message `Command not found`, C-shell cannot find the program in any of the directories specified in the path.

To check your path enter the command:

echo $path

or check your *.login* or *.cshrc* files.

A typical path command looks like the following:

set path = (*/bin /usr/bin /usr/UII/bin $HOME/bin* .)

source *file*   Use to instruct the shell to read or reread *file*. When you enter the command

source *file*

the shell reads (or rereads) the information in *file*. If you have made any changes in your *.login* or *.cshrc* files, you can update your environment by entering the command:

source .login
or
source .cshrc.

By doing this, you do not have to logout and login again to have changes take effect.

Examples:

Sample *.login* file:

```
setenv SHELL /bin/csh
set ignoreeof
set path = (/bin /usr/bin /usr/UII/bin $HOME/bin .)
set noglob
set term = (`tset -m ansi:ansi -m :\?ansi -r -S -Q`)
if ( $status == 0 ) then
    setenv TERM "$term"
end if
unset term noglob
```

.login is executed every time a user logs on.

Sample *.cshrc* file:

```
set noclobber
set history=20
set time=20
if ($?prompt) then
    set prompt=\!%\
# some BSD look-a-likes that maintain a directory stack
    if (! $?_d) set _d = ()
    alias      popd 'cd $_d[1]; echo ${_d[1]}:; shift _d'
    alias      pushd      'set _d = (`pwd` $_d); cd \!*'
    alias      swapd      'set _d = ($_d[2] $_d[1] $_d[3-])'
    alias      flipd      'pushd .; swapd ; popd'
end if
alias print 'pr -n \!:* | lp'        # print command alias
alias cprint 'pr -f -e2 \!:* | lp' # print command alias

# Set 80 /132 char for the terminal qvt 119:

if `tset -` == 'qvt119' then
    alias wide 'setenv TERM qvt119w;tset -r'
    alias small 'setenv TERM qvt119;tset -r'
end if
#
# Set prompt to current directory
#
set cdpath=(.)
set prompt="`pwd` >"
alias cd 'setenv CWD `pwd`; chdir \!:*; set prompt="`pwd` >"'
#
# Defining some aliases
#
alias back 'setenv BACK $CWD; cd $BACK'
alias h history
alias log logout
alias l ls -la
```

.cshrc controls all C-shell environments. Each time you start a shell process, *.cshrc* is executed. It is customary to place all parameters and alias definitions in *.cshrc*.

NOTE:

It is useful to alias your **rm** (remove) command. For example,

```
alias rm 'touch \!* ; mv \!* /u/kentd/.Trash'
```

Instead of removing a file, all subsequent **rm** (remove) commands **touch** the file (changing its date to the current date) and move it (using **mv**) to the directory */u/kentd/.Trash*. Because files are marked with the current date, it is easy to clear them later from *.Trash* using a command like the following.

find */u/kentd/.Trash* **-mtime +3 -exec /bin/rm -f "{}" \;**
This command uses **find** to check */u/kentd/.Trash,* generate a list of files that are more than 3 days old and remove them.

See also:

Bourne shell; Korn shell; App. A-about shell scripts.

---

cut
cutting text from files

    cut cuts out vertical parts of text files. **cut** cuts columns from files and sends the result to the terminal. This command is useful for treating data in tabular -format.

    To be able to use **cut** (and its counterpart **paste**), you have to know how the columns in a given file are separated. Usually the separator is a tab. However, **cut** allows you to use other characters as separators (for example, a ":" or a space).

Command:
    cut *-clist* [*file1 file2* ...]
    cut *-flist* [*file1 file2* ...]
    or
    cut *-flist* [**-d** *delimiter character*] [*file1 file2* ...]

Function:
    Delete or "cut" selected vertical fields in a file.

Options:

-clist	The list following **-c** (no space is allowed) specifies character position, for example **-c1-72** would cut the first 72 characters of each line.
-flist	The list following **-f** specifies a list of fields assumed to be separated in the file by a delimiter character (See **-d**). For example, **-f1,7** means that only the first and the seventh column are cut. Lines with no field delimiters are left intact.
-d *delimiter character*	The character following **-d** is the field separator (**-f** option only). The default field delimiter is tab. If you use a space (or any other character with special meaning to the shell) as the field delimiter, it must be quoted.

        UNIX commands by example

Examples:

Assume you have the following file, *datafile*:

```
Anne:040458:girl:9190.10.24566:Bank of Norway
Starni:040641:boy:8945.43.23457:Bank of Crete
Peter David:22-0759:boy:6072.55.34567:Bank of USA
Vigdis Aasta:090959:girl:2345.72.12675:Bank of Singapore
Nicholas Eric:010356:boy:9180.10.56543.Bank of England
```

datafile consist of 5 fields separated by the field delimiter ":". The five fields are first name, birthday, sex, bank account number, and bank. If we issue the command
cut -f2,5 -d":" *datafile*
cut removes field numbers 2 and 5 in *datafile*. The separator or delimiter is ":". This command produces a screen display similar to the following:

```
040458:Bank of Norway
040641:Bank of Krete
220759:Bank of USA
090959:Bank of Singapore
010356:Bank of England
```

The command
cut -c1-3 *datafile*
gives the first three characters of the first column in the file *datafile*, or:

```
Ann
Sta
Pet
Vig
Nic
```

The following command
cut -d: -f1,5 */etc/passwd*
cuts out the username and the text fields from */etc/passwd*, producing a result resembling the following:

```
root:0000-Admin(0000)
daemon:0000-Admin(0000)
bin:0000-Admin(0000)
sys:0000-Admin(0000)
adm:0000-Admin(0000)
uucp:0000-uucp(0000)
nuucp:0000-uucp(0000)
nobody:uid no body
noaccess:uid no access
lp:0000-LP(0000)
listen:Network Admin
sysadm:general system administration
mhsmail:MHS Admin Processes
david:David Elboth
smtp:SMTP Processes
vigdis:vigdis Enge
```

See also:

grep; paste.

UNIX commands by example

date
set or display system date and time

With **date** you can display or set the date and time.

Command:
date [*mmddhhmm*[*yy*]] [*+format*]

Function:
Displays, formats the display and (if you are *root*) sets date and time. Without arguments, the command **date** gives the date and time.

Options:
The first argument sets the date and time. The argument preceded by a + (second argument above) puts the format of the output of **date** under the control of the user. Both arguments are defined by a set of field codes or descriptors. The abbreviations for the first set of field codes are as follows:

mm	month
dd	date
hh	hours
mm	minutes
yy	year

Any argument to **date** that is preceded by a + sets the format of the output. You can include several field codes. Each one of the field codes sets the conditions for the displayed format. Each field code is separated by a % character.

Format field codes:

n	Forces a line feed.
t	Forces a tab character.
m	The month is used with the format 01 to 12.
d	The date is used with the format 01 to 31.
y	Only the two last digits of the year are included.
H	The hours use the format 00 to 23.
M	The minutes use the format 00 to 59.

S   The seconds use the format 00 to 59.

Examples:

date
Displays the present date and time: for example,

```
Fri Nov 11 11:39:37 EMT 1994
```
(EMT means European Mean Time. If your machine is set for another time zone, you may have different output.)

Most users can only display the date and time. The system administrator can set a new date and time in the system. For example,
date 07291545
Here, the system administrator sets the date to 29 July and the time to 15.45.

The system clock influences all the commands related to time (for example, **cron** jobs). Thus, it is important for the system administrator to make sure that the clock is correctly set and working.

date '+Today's date: %m/%d/%y %nTime: %H:%M:%S'
This command produces:
```
Today's date: 07/13/95
Time: 22:01:49
```

See also:

processes; App. A-about shell scripts.

dd
converting and copying data

dd copies data from one location to another. If necessary, dd can convert data from one input file format to a different output file format. dd can change the byte order, block size, case or character coding (e.g., dd can change EBCDIC to ASCII or vice versa). Most often an input file is copied to an output file. If one or the other is not specified, standard input (instead of an input file) and/or standard output (instead of an output file) are used by default.

dd was developed in order to copy files between different types of file systems and different tape/floppy-formats. Now, several add-on commands using dd are available: for example, the command diskcp (SCO) is used for copying floppies.

Command:
dd [option=*value*] . . .

Function:
Copies data from a specific type of input, or input file, to one of several types of output files.

Options:

if=*file*	Input file name. Standard input is the default.
of=*file*	Output file name. Standard output is the default.
ibs=*n*	Input block size. Specify in *n* bytes (default 512).
obs=*n*	Output block size. Specify in *n* bytes (default 512).
cbs=*n*	Conversion buffer size (logical record length).
bs=*n*	Sets both the input and the output block size. Specify in *n* bytes. This parameter overruns both the **ibs** and the **obs** options.
seek=*n*	Reads the first *n* blocks before starting to copy.

count=*n*	Copies *n* input blocks only.
conv=ascii	Converts from EBCDIC to ASCII.
conv=ebcdic	Converts from ASCII to EBCDIC.
conv=lcase	Converts from capital letters to lowercase. Multibyte characters are not converted.
conv=ucase	Converts from normal letters to uppercase. Multibyte characters are not converted

Examples:

dd if=*/dev/rdsk/f05ht* **of=***/dev/rdsk/f03ht*
Copies everything from a 1.2 Mbyte source floppy to a 1.44 Mbyte target floppy. This is the simplest way of copying programs or data from one floppy format to another.

dd if=*/dev/rfd148ds9* **of=***/dev/rct0*
Copies from a 360 Kbyte source floppy (second disk drive) to tape.

dd if=*/dev/rct0* **of=***/dev/rmt1* **ibs=20k**
Copies from a tape drive (*/dev/rct0*) to an other tape drive (*/dev/rmt1*). The input block size is set to 20 Kbyte.

dd if=*/dev/rct0* **of=***/usr/oracle7/data* **ibs=800 cbs=80 conv=ascii,lcase**
Reads an EBCDIC tape (using */dev/rct0*) blocked into ten 80-byte (conversion buffer size is set to 80 byte) EBCDIC card images per tape block. The input block size is set to 800 bytes. The data from tape are converted to the ASCII file */usr/oracle7/data*. All uppercase letters are converted to lowercase letters. On the disk, data is stored as one single file (*data*).

dd if=/dev/rmt/0h **of=**/tmp/datafile **ibs=800 obs=8K cbs=80 conv=ascii,ucase**
Reads an EBCDIC tape (using /dev/rmt/0h) blocked into ten 80-byte (conversion buffer size is set to 80 bytes) images per record into the ASCII file /tmp/datafile. The output block size (**cbs** or conversion buffer size) is set to 8 Kbytes. All lower-case letters are converted to uppercase letters. On the disk all the data is stored as one single file (datafile).

With **bs** you can specify the block size (in bytes) in either **k** , **b**, or **w**. **k** specifies 1024 bytes, **b** specifies 512 bytes and **w** specifies 2 bytes. For example, if you wanted to copy the file, filename, to a 1.44 Mb floppy, with an input and output block size of 20 Kbytes, you might enter the command
dd if=file **of=**/dev/rfd0135ds18 **bs=20K**

Similarly, to copy 400 1 Kbyte blocks from a file system placed at /dev/rhd0 to tape /dev/rct0, we might enter:
dd if=/dev/rhd0 **of=**/dev/rct0 **bs=1K count=400**
Note that the **bs** command sets block size to 1 Kbyte (1024 bytes) for both the input **and** output files.

See also:

Backing up UNIX systems; copy; cp; cpio; restore; tar.

df
listing free disk space

df lists the number of free blocks and inodes on a file system.

Command:
df [-i] [-a] [-t] [*filesystem*]

Function:
Shows the number of free blocks and inodes in a file system. The displayed sizes are reported in number of blocks. Normally, a block is 512 bytes (1 Kbyte is 1024 bytes or 2 blocks).

Options:

    -a   Reports on all file systems including ones which have zero total blocks (Only Solaris and UnixWare).

    -t   Reports the total number of free and used blocks and inodes(SCO, Solaris and UnixWare).

    -i   Displays percentage of used and unused inodes (Only SCO and UnixWare).

Arguments:
filesystem   Any filesystem you want to specify

The **df** command without arguments displays the number of free blocks and inodes in all currently mounted local file systems. On SCO UNIX systems, the command **dfspace** displays the number of free Mbytes.

Examples:

(UnixWare)

If you issue the command **df**, you will see output resembling the following:

```
/              (/dev/root        ):   19176 blocks   19912 files
/proc          (/proc            ):       0 blocks     165 files
/dev/fd        (/dev/fd          ):       0 blocks       0 files
/stand         (/dev/dsk/c0t0d0sa):   3196 blocks      98 files
```

The **-a** option produces reports on used and available space as well as the device driver name for all file systems including the ones which have zero total blocks. To determine how many Kbytes remain, divide the total blocks by 2. To obtain the number of megabytes, divide the total Kbytes by 1024. The formula is as follows:

Blocks/2=KBytes Kbytes/1024=Mbytes

(Solaris)

The command

df -a

produces output resembling the following:

File system	kbytes	used	avail	capacity	Mounted on
/dev/dsk/c0t3d0s0	17095	12736	2659	83%	/
/dev/dsk/c0t3d0s6	162286	145770	296	100%	/us
/proc	0	0	0	0%	/proc
fd	0	0	0	0%	/dev/fd
swap	72248	716	71532	1%	/tmp
/dev/dsk/c0t3d0s3	200430	131	80377	0%	/export
/dev/dsk/c0t3d0s7	7355	9	6616	0	/export/home
/dev/dsk/c0t3d0s5	38115	33309	996	97%	/opt
david:(pid141)	0	0	0	0%	/net
david:(pid141)	0	0	0	0%	/home

Files:

/dev/* /etc/mnttab

The **df** command uses various programs, depending on the file system in question. Some of those programs are found in the directory */etc/fscmd.d/**filesystemtype***.

Directories
using UNIX directories

Directories - groups of files

A directory is an index to the files stored on a disk or portion of a disk. A disk's contents are not readily apparent. A directory is how files appear to UNIX. Under UNIX the complete or absolute filename is specified by the complete path name, e.g., */usr/david/payroll*. The path consists of the file system (in this case the root filesystem or */*), the directories *usr* and *david*. *payroll* specifies the filename. If the path does not start with a */*, the filename is relative to the user's current position in the filesystem. In that case, the system starts to search for a file from the directory where the user is situated.

The UNIX hierarchical file system

UNIX uses a hierarchical file system (tree structure) for organizing its files. Each system directory has a function. The UNIX kernel is stored with the filename *unix*. SCO UNIX stores the kernel in the *root* directory(or */*). If you are using Solaris, the UNIX kernel is stored under *root* as a separate file system (*/unix*). If you are using UnixWare, the UNIX kernel is placed in a separate filesystem (*/stand/unix*).

Each user has their own disk area where all the user files and directories are stored. These user areas are usually set up as directories below */home*, */usr*, */usr1*, */usr2*, */u*, */u1*, */u2*, etc. Usually, *home*, *usr1*, *u*, *u1*, etc. are separate filesystems.

For example, user David's files are placed under */usr/david* or */u/david*, and Jane's files are placed under */home/jane*, */usr/jane* or */u/jane*.

A directory may contain one or more subdirectories or files. *root* has the following system directories:

/bin   UNIX commands. In this directory are the UNIX system commands. These may be UNIX commands or UNIX batch routines. Some of the most familiar commands in this directory are

basename	echo	passwd	su
cp	expr	rm	sync
date	fsck	sh	tar
dump	login	sleep	restore
dumpdir	mv	stty	test

/dev   */dev* contains several subdirectories, which contain device drivers for hard disks, floppy drives, tape drives, screens etc. For example, */dev/dsk* and */dev/rdsk* contain device drivers for floppy drives and hard disks. UnixWare has tape and CD ROM drivers in the directories */dev/rmt* and */dev/cdrom*. Unlike Solaris, SCO UNIX and UnixWare support AT&T conventions for naming the device drivers. Where relevant, the files in */dev/dsk* and */dev/rdsk* are linked to the devices in */dev*.

/etc   Administration directory. Contains the files, scripts and tables for system administration. None of the files in this directory should be removed.

/lib   Libraries used by the UNIX operating system.

/mnt   Temporary mount-directory. The */mnt* directory is an empty directory reserved for temporarily connecting file systems.

/usr   User routines or user area. */usr* contains user accounts and applications.

/tcb   System files for TCB (Trusted Computing Base). These directories contain programs making SCO UNIX C-2 secure (only relevant for SCO UNIX).

/tmp   Temporary files. Stores temporary files. This means files with a short lifetime. */tmp* files are usually connected with a program or binary. If the program or binary is aborted, the temporary files should be removed. Temporary files may be removed if they do not belong to a running program.

All of the above directories (except */tcb*) are necessary to UNIX systems. SCO UNIX UnixWare and Solaris may also have these system directories:

/boot	boot-time files
/home	user home directories
/home2	user home directories
/install	add-on packages
/opt	add-on material
/proc	current processes
/sbin	administrative bin
/shlib	shared libraries
/stand	UNIX kernel and boot-time files (only UnixWare)
./NetWare	mount point for NetWare servers (only UnixWare)
/usr/X	X Windows System support
/usr/add-on	support files for add-on packages
/usr/ccs	C compilation system
/usr/lbin	local bin
/usr/lib/*	different directories
/usr/net	control files for **nfs** and RFS (Remote File System)
/usr/nserve	RFS administration (Solaris only)
/usr/sadm	system administration
/var	files that change
/var/adm	accounting control
/var/lp	logs for **lp**
/var/sadm	system administration support files
/var/spool	temporary files for **print** and **uucp**
/var/uucp	logs for **uucp**

DOS
using DOS with UNIX

Most Intel-chip-based UNIX systems provide some level of DOS support. Most support some DOS commands. Others allow you to mount and manipulate DOS file systems. However, the names of the commands may vary. The commands and examples in this chapter are based on SCO UNIX and UnixWare.

NOTE:

SCO UNIX, Solaris and UnixWare are available with a DOS emulator (e.g., Locus Computing Corporation's Merge 386™). If your version of UNIX is equipped with a DOS emulator, it is often easier and better to use actual DOS or DR.DOS™ commands supplied with the emulator rather than their UNIX equivalents.

SCO UNIX and UnixWare have commands that can be used to manipulate DOS files on DOS diskettes and DOS partitions (hard disks in DOS format). Solaris 2.x supports the formatting of DOS diskettes with the **format** command. All commands under SCO and UnixWare for using DOS have DOS in the name. For example, if the defaults have been set correctly, **dosdir** *a:* (or, if the defaults have not been set, **dosdir** */dev/fd0*) displays the contents of the root directory of the DOS disk in the first floppy drive. Commands for working with DOS file systems have the same names under SCO UNIX and UnixWare.

DOS files are accessed by specifying the name of the driver, for example, */dev/rfd0/**filename***. You can change the default driver for DOS disks by examining the system default file, */etc/default/msdos* (SCO and UnixWare only). For example, to set your DOS floppy drive *A:* to be the same as your first UNIX floppy drive (*/dev/fd0*), you must place the line:

```
A=/dev/fd0
```

in */etc/default/msdos*.

Here is an example of */etc/default/msdos*:

```
# @(#) default.src 23.1 91/08/29
#
# Copyright (C) 1986-1991 The Santa Cruz Operation, Inc.
#           All Rights Reserved.
# The information in this file is provided for the exclusive
# use of the licensees of The Santa Cruz Operation, Inc.
# Such users have the right to use, modify, and incorporate
# this code into other products for purposes authorized by
# the license agreement provided they include this notice
# and the associated copyright notice with any such product.
# The information in this file is provided "AS IS" without
# warranty.
# Floppy device names
A=/dev/rfd0
B=/dev/rfd1
# Hard disk drives
C=/dev/hd0d
D=/dev/hd1d
```

It is important to remember that DOS text files use a carriage return-line feed at the end of each line (CR-LF); UNIX files use only the LF. Thus, when converting files from one environment to the other you must convert the line feed characters. By default, **doscp** and **doscat** add or strip (depending on the direction of the transfer) the line-feed characters. Options are provided with each command enabling the user to override the defaults.

doscat - DOS file contents

Command:
doscat [-r] [-m] *file* ...

Function:
Displays the contents of a DOS file on the screen.

Options:
-r   The file is displayed without line-feed conversion.

-m   The file is displayed with new line conversion.

Arguments:

file   The name of one or more DOS files. Note that wildcards are not
                supported.

Examples:

doscat *a:config.sys*
Displays the content of the DOS file *config.sys*. The file is stored on the first floppy
diskette.

doscat */dev/fd0:letter.txt*
Also displays the content of a DOS file, in this case the file *letter.txt*. This file is
also stored on the first floppy diskette, but instead of using the DOS designation *a:*,
we use the UNIX driver, */dev/fd0:*.

---

doscp - copying a DOS file

Command:
    doscp [-r] [-m] *file1 file2*
    or
    doscp [-r] [-m] *file1...directory*

Function:
    Copies files to and from a DOS partition or floppy and a UNIX file system.

Options:
    -r   The file is copied without line-feed conversion.

    -m   The file is copied with new line conversion.

Arguments:
    file1:   Name of the source file.
    file2:   Name of the target file.
    directory   Name of the target directory.

Examples:

doscp *test a:\test*
Copies the file *test* from the current directory to the root directory on the DOS drive
A:.

doscp *a:test test*
Reverses the previous command. Copies the file *test* from the current directory on
DOS drive *A* to the current directory on the UNIX file system.

doscp */tmp/test /dev/fd0:datafile*
Copies */tmp/test* to the root directory on drive *A:* and changes the filename to
datafile. Note that the command uses the UNIX driver name for the floppy drive
instead of *A:*.

doscp */dev/fd0:datafile /tmp/test*
Reverses the previous command. Copies */dev/fd0:datafile* from the current directory
on drive *A:* to the UNIX file system and changes the name to */tmp/test*.

doscp */home/letter1 /home/letter2 /dev/fd1:/mydir*
Copies two files (*/home/letter1* and */home/letter2*) to the directory */mydir* on the
second UNIX floppy drive (normally DOS drive *B:*).

dosdir - DOS directory listing in DOS format

Command:
dosdir *drive* or *directory* ...

Function:
Displays the content of a DOS partition or floppy drive in DOS format.

Options:
No options.

Arguments:

directory	one or more DOS directories
drive	DOS floppy drive.

Examples:

dosdir *a:*
Displays the contents of the first floppy drive (usually *A:*).

dosdir *c:*
Displays the contents of the primary DOS partition (usually drive *C:*). Note that if you have mounted the DOS file system, this command will return a `device busy` error.

dosdir */dev/fd0:/util*
Displays the contents of the *A:\util*.

dosls - DOS directory listing in UNIX format

Command:
dosls *directory* ...

Function:
Displays the contents of a DOS floppy or partition in UNIX format.

Options:
No options.

Arguments:
directory: One or more DOS directories.

With **dosls**, directory information is displayed in UNIX **ls** format.

dosrm - removing a DOS file

Command:
    dosrm *devicename:..filename*

Function:
    Removes a DOS file from a DOS floppy or partition.

Options:
    No options.

Arguments:
    devicename   Name of the DOS device.
    filename   Name of the file(s) to be removed.

Examples:

dosrm */dev/fd0:/wp/printer/print.tst*
Removes the file */wp/printer/print.tst* from the first floppy drive (usually *A:*).

> **dosrm** *a:autoexec.bat*
> Removes the file *autoexec.bat* from the first UNIX floppy drive.

dosmkdir - creating a DOS directory

Command:
dosmkdir *devicename directory* ...

Function:
Creates a directory on a DOS partition or floppy drive.

Options:
No options.

Arguments:
devicename Name of device that will hold the directory.
directory: Name of the DOS directory to be created.

Examples:

dosmkdir *C:/batch*
Creates a subdirectory */batch* on the primary DOS partition (usually *C:*). Note that if you have mounted the DOS filesystem, this command will return a `device busy` error.

dosmkdir */dev/fd0:/wp/doc*
This command creates a subdirectory (*/wp/doc*) n DOS partition A.

dosrmdir - removing a DOS directory

Command:
dosrmdir *devicename directory*

Function:
Removes a directory on a DOS partition or floppy drive.

Options:
No options.

Arguments:
devicename   Name of device that holds the directory to be removed.
directory: Name of the DOS directory to be removed.

Examples:

dosrmdir *c:/batch*
Removes */batch* from the primary DOS partition (usually *C:*). Note that if you have mounted the DOS filesystem, this command will return a `device busy` error.

dosrmdir */dev/fd0:/wp/doc*
The command removes */wp/doc* from the first UNIX floppy drive (usually *A:*).

dosformat - formatting a DOS diskette

Command:
dosformat [-fqv] *devicename*

Function:
Formats a diskette in DOS format (usually in DOS 2.0 format). Note that **dosformat** cannot be used to format a hard disk. To format a DOS partition on a hard disk, you must first boot DOS and use the DOS **format** command.

Options:

-f   Suppresses interactive features.

-q   Quiet-suppresses systems messages to screen.

-v   Requests volume label, i.e., the name of the diskette after formatting.

Arguments:

devicename   Name of the floppy device DOS (if defined in */etc/default/msdos*) or UNIX format.

Examples:

dosformat */dev/fd0*
Formats a floppy disk in the first floppy device (usually *A:*).

dosformat *b:*
If the device is defined in */etc/default/msdos*, formats a floppy disk in the second UNIX floppy device.

Solaris 2.x formats DOS floppy disks with the command **fdformat**. For example, the command
fdformat -d
is equivalent to using the DOS format command.

du
amount of disk space in use

du displays the amount of disk space (in 512-byte blocks) used by each subdirectory in a named directory. The current working directory is the default. A system administrator can use the **du** command to find out which users consume space on the system's hard disk.

The report can be a bit misleading. For example, if a user has files of 1 byte and 513 bytes, they appear to be 1 and 2 blocks respectively. If too many files are linked, **du** will count the extra files more than once.

To convert blocks to Kbytes or Mbytes, divide the total blocks by 2. That will give you the number of Kbytes. To obtain the number of megabytes, divide the total Kbytes by 1024. The formula is the following:

Blocks/2 = Kbytes   Kbytes/1024 = Mbytes

On most UNIX systems, **du** uses a block size of 512 bytes. However, on some systems, it may use 1024 bytes (1 Kbyte), 2048 bytes (2 Kbytes) or 4096 bytes (4 Kbytes). Check your user documentation to determine which block size your system uses.

Command:
du [-ars] [*directory*]

Function:
Reports the disk space used by files and directories in a named directory.

Options:

-a   Report on the number of blocks for each file.

-r   Gives error message if files and directories cannot be opened or read.

-s   Reports a summary total only for the specified directory.

Arguments:

Without any options, **du** reports the number of blocks recursively for the current working directory and every directory below the current directory. If you specify the directory name as an argument to the command, the system displays a view of the area used by the directory and all subdirectories.

Examples:

If there are no subdirectories, **du** with no options produces the following:

```
du
124
```

`124` represents the number of blocks in use in the current working directory.

The command
   du -a
produces the following:

```
2          ././.profile
2          ././.vtlrc
2          ././.vtlrc.els
4          ././.sh_history
2          ./fileset
2          ./fileset
2          ./kap4
52         ./kap11
52         ./test
2          ./post
0          ./letter
124        .
```

The numbers represent the usage of blocks for each directory. The last number gives the total usage.

echo
echo to the screen

echo displays its argument, separated by a space and terminated by a line feed. echo may also be specified with special types of codes.

Command:
echo [*argument*]

Function:
Sends a string of text or code to the screen.

Arguments:
-*string*   A character string that may include escape sequences inside quotation marks. A few of the supported sequences are the following:

\b	Backspace
\c	Print without newline character
\f	Form feed
\n	Newline
\r	Return
\x	Where x\ is any octal number

For a complete review of the sequences supported by your UNIX system, see your **echo** manual page.

Arguments may be text and/or code or wildcards. The command used without any arguments sends an empty string to the screen.

Examples:

echo Hello
Sends the text string "Hello" to the screen.

echo Good morning
Sends the text string "Good morning" to the screen.

You can send a character from the ASCII- or ISO-table by giving the octal code. For example,

echo "\07"
Sends the code **<Ctrl-g>** to the screen.

echo "\063"
Sends the number 3 to the screen.

echo "\0101"
Sends the letter A to the screen.

echo "Hello, how are you!! \c"
Sends the text string Hello, how are you!! to the screen, without including line feed.

echo *
Functions like the **ls** command. It lists the files in the current directory.

See also:

sh; ls.

/etc/passwd and /etc/group
defining users

Before you can log in to a UNIX terminal or console, many processes must already be running. The procedure begins with **init,** the parent process of all the **getty**s (get tty input). The **getty** program makes ongoing polls of each terminal. When **init** receives a valid user name and password, it starts a shell and displays the message of the day. In order for the user name and the password to make any sense, **init** must check to ensure that the user name and the password are valid. The most important files to that login process are */etc/passwd* and */etc/group*.

/etc/passwd defines valid login names as well as passwords and command shells. The user's group file permissions are defined in */etc/group*.

The columns in the password file have the following fields:

user name	The user name is defined by the system administrator. The user name should, as a rule, consist only of lowercase letters.
password	The next field is the password. On most systems this field is also set up to have additional functions. If a user must change passwords at next login or if a password has expired, this case can be specified with a certain code in the field. On most systems the field containing the user's password is encrypted. This case is, as a rule, marked by an x. The encrypted password itself is placed in a separate file (usually */etc/shadow*).
user number	The user number is a unique number pointing to the user name.
group number	The group number indicates which groups the user is member of. The names of the groups are found in */etc/group*.
text field	On most systems, the text field in */etc/passwd* can be at most 38 characters long. This field might contain a text

UNIX commands by example

description of pertinent information about the user, for example, user's full name.

user area

The user area shows the location of the user's working area. For example, */usr/philip*, */usr2/anne*, */u/laura*, */home/peter*, */users/hartley*.

shell

The shell is an interactive program functioning as a command interpreter. The following abbreviations in */etc/passwd* mean:

csh   C-shell
sh   Bourne shell
rsh   Restricted shell
ksh   Korn shell

Example of */etc/passwd*:

```
root:x:0:3:0000-Admin(0000):/:/sbin/sh
daemon:x:1:12:0000-Admin(0000):/:
bin:x:2:2:0000-Admin(0000):/usr/bin:
sys:x:3:3:0000-Admin(0000):/:
adm:x:4:4:0000-Admin(0000):/var/adm:
uucp:x:5:5:0000-uucp(0000):/usr/lib/uucp:
nobody:x:60001:60001:uid no body:/:
noaccess:x:60002:60002:uid no access:/:
lp:x:7:9:0000-LP(0000):/var/spool/lp:/sbin/sh
listen:x:37:4:Network Admin:/usr/net/nls:/usr/bin/sh
sysadm:x:0:0:general system
administration:/usr/sadm:/usr/sbin/sysadm
mhsmail:x:61:6:MHS Admin Processes:/var/spool/smf:/usr/bin/sh
david:x:202:1:David Elboth:/home/david:/usr/bin/sh
smtp:x:100:6:SMTP Processes:/var/spool/smtpq:/usr/bin/sh
vigdis:x:101:1:vigdis Enge:/home/vigdis:/usr/bin/ksh
```

In the above example, `david` is the name of a user. Instead of seeing an encrypted password, you see only one single `x` for all users. If you do not have the encrypting key, you cannot find the password. You find the encrypted password in the file */etc/shadow*. The number `202` is the user number assigned to david.
The number `1` points to a group. To find the name of the group, look in the file */etc/group*. The descriptive text string for `david`, is "David Elboth." The descriptive field can contain up to 38 characters.
The working area is defined as */home/david* and the shell `david` uses is the Bourne shell (*/usr/bin/sh*). The user `vigdis` uses the Korn shell (*/usr/bin/ksh*).

Note that the system administrator has user number 0 and uses the Bourne shell.

Example of */etc/shadow:*

```
root:6o.mgynXy0ywY:8400:0:168:7:::
daemon:NP:6445::::::
bin:NP:6445::::::
sys:NP:6445::::::
adm:NP:6445::::::
uucp:NP:6445::::::
nuucp:NP:6445::::::
nobody:NP:6445::::::
noaccess:NP:6445::::::
lp:*LK*:::::::
listen:*LK*:::::::
sysadm:Ko2ofGZwrrD82:8400:0:168:7:::
mhsmail:*LK*:::::::
david:SmIi/1MF9.72w:8570:0:168:7:::
smtp:*LK*:::::::
vigdis:T3/qU.O1pKloM:8549::::::
```

Example of */etc/group*:

```
root::0:root
other::1:root
bin::2:root,bin,daemon
sys::3:root,bin,sys,adm
adm::4:root,adm,daemon
uucp::5:root,uucp
mail::6:root
tty::7:root,tty,adm
```

```
audit::8:root
nuucp::10:root,nuucp
daemon::12:root,daemon
cron::23:root
priv::47:root
nobody::60001:
noaccess::60002:
lp::9:root,lp
dos::100:
```

/etc/group has the following fields:
-group name
-group number
-members of the group

Users can change their group by means of the **newgrp** command. For example. if there is a group with the name "word", the command
   newgrp word
changes the user's group to word.

See also:

Bourne shell; C-shell; Korn shell; passwd.

fdformat
formatting floppy disks

With **fdformat** you can format diskettes for use on your Solaris 2.x UNIX system; you can also format floppy disks for use with DOS. (SCO UNIX and Unix-Ware use **format** and **dosformat** to format floppy disks. See **dosformat** and **format** for more information).

Command:
fdformat [-dev] [**L** or **l**] [-**b** *label*] [*floppydrive*]

Function:
Format floppy disks for use on a Solaris 2.x system.

Options:

-d   Formats floppy disk for DOS use.

-e   Forces disk to eject after formatting.

-v   Verifies that the disk is error-free after format is completed.

-L or l   Formats a low density floppy disk (720 Kbyte). Suppresses normally displayed information about the track/sector or error messages.

-b *label*   Puts a DOS volume label on the disk after formatting it (only works with the **-d** option).

floppydrive   The name of the floppy device.

UNIX commands by example

Examples:

Solaris (Sunsoft) floppy diskette names are *diskette* or *rdiskette* and are linked to devices constructed as follows:

rfd0 { a | b | c ...}

Standard sector size is 512 bytes per sector. If you want to specify a raw (character) device, include the *r* (**format** */dev/rdiskette*) in the device name.

fdformat */dev/diskette*
Formats a 1.44 Mbyte 3.5" diskette placed in the floppy drive.

fdformat */dev/rdiskette*
Uses the raw (character) device to format a 1.44 Mbyte floppy in the floppy drive.

fdformat - l */dev/rdiskette*
Formats a low density 720 Kbyte 3.5" floppy placed in the floppy drive.

On Solaris 2.x workstations, you must use the command **eject** when you want to eject the diskette. You can also specify the - **e** option to the format command. For example,
fdformat - **e** */dev/diskette*
formats and then ejects a 1.44 Mbyte 3.5" floppy placed in the floppy drive.

Files:
The device drivers are placed in */dev/** and */dev/rdsk/**.

Solaris uses */dev/rfd0, /dev/rfd0c, /dev/diskette* and */dev/rdiskette* to specify default formatting parameters.

See also:
dosformat; format.

file
determining file type

If you don't know the type of a given file, you can use **file** to determine its type. This command executes a series of tests. The **file** command uses the file */etc/magic* to determine the "magic number" of a file. That number is then equated with a file type. Several formats are recognized.

Command:
  file [-m *filename*] [-f *filename*] *filename*

Function:

  Determines file type.

Options:
  -m *filename* Causes **file** to use *filename* as an alternate to */etc/magic*.

  -f *filename* Causes **file** to examine all the files listed in *filename.*

Arguments:
  filename **file** requires a filename as an argument. **file** recognizes wildcards. If you use **file** without any options, *filename* is analyzed to determine the file type.

File types

ASCII text	Text files where less then 20% of the commands are terminated by a space or a line feed
c program text	C source program
commands text	Shell program
directory	Directory
empty	Empty file
data	Standard data file

Examples:

If you were to issue the command:

file *

you would see output similar to the following:

```
batch:          commands text
c-files:        directory
cls.bat:        commands text
cls.c:          c program text
convert.c:      c program text
fil:            empty
ifs:            commands text
test:           directory
uni.c:          c program text
uniconv.c:      c program text
```

Files
UNIX filenames, types and permissions

File names

Current versions of UNIX (SCO UNIX 3.2.4, UnixWare 1.2 and Solaris 2.3 and newer) support filenames up to 256 characters long. Some older UNIX variants only handle 14 characters. With UNIX, unlike DOS, you can use one or more dots at any place in the filename.

The following filename rules apply:

- The filename can consist of a maximum of 256 characters
- The following special characters are used by UNIX commands and therefore cannot be used in filenames:
  ( ) { } ? [ ] < > ; | ' ` " \ &
- Similarly, neither spaces nor control characters can be used in filenames.
- Although most filenames are lowercase, UNIX is case sensitive.

All system files (files necessary for defining your user environment) are prefixed by a dot ("."). Thus, your home directory has files such as *.profile*, *.login*, *.cshrc*, and *.kshrc*. By default, these files are not shown by most UNIX file list commands (e.g., **ls**) unless you specify an option requiring that they be displayed (e.g., **ls -a**). If you wish to "hide" a file in this way, you can prefix the filename by a dot, for example *.lettername*.

Any user who creates a file or directory, will automatically be the owner of this file or directory. The owner of a file or directory can decide who may have access to that file.

Three types of access privileges can be set:
- Read access
- Write access
- Execute access (or search in a directory)

The access rights are set independently for each of the four categories of users: u, g, o and a.

The user categories are:

u   user

g   group
o   other
a   all

For more information on changing access rights or ownership, see **chmod**, **chgrp** and **chown** .

Using wildcards

UNIX supports the use of the following special characters as wildcards in file or directory names:

   ?   denotes any simple character
   *   denotes any group of characters
   [ ]   represents characters or intervals (with use of hyphen)

In place of a wildcard character, UNIX inserts other characters, according to the rules shown below. With the help of wildcards, you may specify names for one file or directory, or alternatively, for a group of files and directories.

Wildcards can be combined with each other or with any other characters to produce a desired result.

Below are a few examples of how to use wildcards with the **ls** command together with a short description of what the commands would return:

ls *   Lists all the files in the current directory.

ls f*   Lists all the files in the current directory with names starting with an f.

ls *.o   Lists all the files in the current directory with names ending in o.

ls ???   Lists all the files in the current directory consisting of exactly 3 characters.

ls chap?   Lists all the files in the current directory prefixed by chap and which contain one additional character, for example *chapa*, *chapb*, *chap4*.

ls chap[1-4] Lists all the files in the current directory that begin with chap and have either 1, 2, 3. or 4 following. Includes *chap1*, *chap2*, *chap3* and *chap4*.

ls [kc]hap Lists all the files in the current directory that begin with either k or c and end with hap, e.g., chap or khap.

Wildcards can be used with most UNIX file-handling commands, but they must be used carefully. For example, **rm** * removes all the files in the current working directory.

Note that if you place wildcards in quotations, either single (")or double(""), UNIX views the wildcard as a regular character.

File listings

File listings display varying degrees of information about files. For example, the command:

ls - la

results in output resembling the following:

```
total 24
drwx------    6 david     Support     272 Oct 27 03:46 .
drwxrwxr-x   22 root      auth        352 Oct 25 14:19 ..
-rw-------    1 david     Support    2080 Nov 11  1988 .cshrc
-rw-------    1 david     Support     884 Nov 10  1988 .login
drwxr-xr-x    2 david     group       176 Oct 19 12:01 UII
drwxrwxrwx    2 david     group       720 Oct 22 22:35 batch
drwxr-xr-x    2 david     group       160 Oct 22 22:34 files
-rw-rw-r--    1 david     Support     365 Oct 26 00:44 group
-rw-rw-r--    1 david     Support     881 Oct 26 00:44 passwd
-rw-r--r--    1 david     Support     544 Oct 27 03:46 text
```

The first column (e.g., `drwxrw--`) displays a description of the file type and permissions. The second column displays the number of links. The third and fourth column display the owner and group (see chgrp; chmod and chown). The next two columns display the size and creation time. The last column contains the name of the file or directory.

See also:

chgrp; chmod; chown; directories; file.

find
finding files

find is a powerful tool for finding files anywhere in a UNIX file system. It is often used as a "front-end" to produce output for other UNIX commands (e.g., **cpio**) With **find**, you can find a particular file or set of files within the file system. Several search criteria can be specified. Among them are filename, inode number of the file, file owner, file group, file date and file size.

Command:
find *directory options* [*filename*] [*expression*]
or put more generally,
find where what expression

Function:
Finds files using user-defined selection criteria.

Options:

-name *filename*	True if file is identical to filename.
-user *user name*	True if file belongs to user name.
-group *name*	True if file belongs to group name.
-size *n*	True if size is *n*. *n* is number of blocks (one block = 512 bytes).
-atime *n*	True if the file has been used *n* days ago.
-exec *command*	True if the executed command returns a zero value as exit status. The end of *command* must be punctuated by an escaped semicolon (e.g., \;).
-print	Displays the search path.

-o	**-o** is used in arguments to the **find** command to indicate "and/or". That is, **-o** indicates that a given option should be executed if either or both arguments to a **find** command are true.

Arguments:

directory	*directory* tells **find** where to start looking for a file or object. By default, **find** searches recursively from the specified *directory*.

If no criteria are used, the **find** command will not produce a result.

Examples:

find . -name *letter* **-print**
The "." means that the search is done in the current directory. The expression **-name** *letter* specifies a search for the file named *letter*. If *letter* is found, **print** displays the search path.

find / -name *unixbook* **-print**
Searches recursively for the file *unixbook* from *root* (/) through the entire file structure. If *unixbook* is found, **print** displays the search path.

find */home* **-name** *letter1* **-print**
Searches recursively for the file *letter1* starting in the directory */home*. If the file is found, **print** displays the search path.

find / -user david -print
Searches recursively for all files belonging to david. If any are found, **print** displays the search path.

find / -atime +2 -print
Searches recursively for all files that have been in use the last two days. If any are found, **print** displays the search path.

find . -size 0 -print
Searches in current directory for all files with zero size. If any are found, **print** displays the search path.

find / -name *wp* **-exec ls -l {} \;**
Searches recursively for all files named *wp*. For all files found, executes **ls -l.** The curly braces ({ }) indicate that the command should insert the path name of the found files. The escaped semicolon (\;) terminates the command.

find */usr/david* **-name** *left** **-print**
Searches recursively from */usr/david* for all files that start with *left*.

The following is a complex example of a **find** command:

find / \(-name core -o -name "*.out" \) -atime +7 -exec rm {} \;
This command first finds all files named *core* and/or with the file extension *.out* that have been accessed in last seven days and then removes them. Note that the two **name** options are joined by **-o,** indicating that **find** should find files satisfying either or both conditions. Also note that when two commands are joined, they are enclosed in escaped parentheses [e.g., \(, \)].

format
formatting floppy disks

With **format** (SCO UNIX and UnixWare) and **fdformat** (Solaris 2.x), you can format diskettes for use on your UNIX system. With the **fdformat** command you can also format floppies for use with DOS. The two commands have different options.

Command:
format [**-f**] [**-q**] [**-v**] [**-i** *interleave*] *floppydrive*

Function:
Format floppies for use under UNIX.

Options:

-f   Turns off the interactive feature.

-q   (quiet) Suppresses normally displayed information about the track/sector or error messages.

-v   Verifies that the disk is error free after format is completed.

-i *interleave*   Specifies the interleave factor.

floppydrive   Specifies the name of the floppy device. If the device driver is not specified, the format program uses the default specified in */etc/default/format* (for example, */dev/rfd0*).

Examples:

UnixWare:
UnixWare floppy diskette names are constructed as follows:

fx { *5h* | *5d9* | *5d8* | *5d4* | *5d16* | *5q* | *3h* | *3 d*}*t*

The middle part of a floppy diskette name gives information about the format parameters (density) of this device:

Format parameters

5h	high density (1.2 Mbyte 5.25" floppy, 80 cylinders, 2-sided)
5d9	double density, 9 sectors per track (360 Kbyte 5.25" floppy, 40 cylinders, 2-sided)
5d8	double density, 8 sectors per track (320 Kbyte 5.25" floppy, 40 cylinders, 2-sided)
5d4	double density, 4 sectors per track 1024 bytes per sector (320 Kbyte 5.25" floppy, 40 cylinders, 2-sided)
5d15	double density, 16 sectors per track 256 bytes per sector (320 Kbyte 5.25" floppy, 40 cylinders, 2-sided)
5q	quad density, 9 sectors per track (730 Kbyte 5.25" floppy, 80 cylinders, 2-sided)
3h	high density (1.44 Mbyte 3.5" floppy, 80 cylinders, 2-sided)
3d	quad density (730 Kbyte 3.5" floppy, 80 cylinders, 2-sided)

Standard sector size is 512 bytes per sector (exceptions to this are 5d4 and 5d16, as noted in the above list). The optional t, appended to the device name, shows whether this device makes use of the complete floppy diskette (the t then is part of the device name) or if the first cylinder of the floppy diskette is not to be used (there is no t in the device name). x is either 0 (A) or 1 (B), depending on which drive you want to access.

UnixWare command examples:

format */dev/rdsk/f03ht*
Formats a 1.44 Mbyte 3.5" floppy placed in the first floppy drive.

format */dev/rdsk/f15ht*
Formats a 1.2 Mbyte 5.25" floppy placed in the second floppy drive.

format */dev/rdsk/f05q*
Formats a quad density 720 Kbyte 5.25" floppy placed in the first floppy drive.

format */dev/rdsk/f05d9*
Formats 360 Kbyte 5.25" floppy placed in the first floppy drive.

SCO UNIX:
SCO UNIX floppy diskette names are constructed as follows:

[r]fdx {96ds15 | 96ds9 | 96ss15 | 48ds9 | 48ds8 | 48ss9 | 48ss8 | 135ss18 | 135ds18}

Standard sector size is 512 bytes per sector. *x* signifies the floppy drive. *x* can have a value of 0 (usually corresponds to the DOS A: drive) or 1 (usually corresponds to the DOS B: drive). Which you use depends on which drive you want to access. To specify a raw (character) device, include the *r* (e.g., format */dev/rfd048ds9*) in the device name.

The middle part of a floppy diskette name gives information about the format parameters of the device:

Format parameters

48ss8	double density, 8 sectors per track (160 Kbyte 5.25" floppy, 40 cylinders, 1-sided)
48ss9	double density, 9 sectors per track (180 Kbyte 5.25" floppy, 40 cylinders, 1-sided)
48ds8	double density, 8 sectors per track (320 Kbyte 5.25" floppy, 40 cylinders, 2-sided)
48ds9	double density, 9 sectors per track (360 Kbyte 5.25" floppy, 40 cylinders, 2-sided)
96ds9	quad density (720 Kbyte 5.25" floppy, 80 cylinders, 2-sided)
96ds15	high density (1.2 Mbyte 5.25" floppy, 80 cylinders, 2-sided)
135ds9	high density, 18 sectors per track (720 Kbyte 3.5" floppy, 80 cylinders, 1-sided)
135ds18	quad density, 18 sectors per track (1.44 Mbyte 3.5" floppy 2-sided)

SCO UNIX command examples

format
Formats the drive specified in */etc/default/format*. That file can also be used to require that the disk be verified after formatting.

format */dev/rfd0*
Formats a disk placed in the first floppy drive (*/dev/rfd0*). The device driver points to the driver (e.g. */dev/rfd096ds15* 1.2 MB) for the first floppy drive (usually equivalent to DOS A:).

format */dev/rfd048ds9*
Formats a 360 Kbyte 5.25" diskette in the first floppy drive.

format */dev/rfd096ds15*
Formats a 1.2 Mbyte 5.25" diskette in the first floppy drive.

format -v */dev/rfd196ss15*
Formats a 600 Kbyte 5.25" floppy in the second floppy drive. The diskette is formatted on one side only (ss = single side). The **-v** option means that all tracks and sectors are verified.

format */dev/rfd196ds15*
Formats a 1.2 Mbyte 5.25" floppy placed in the second floppy drive.

format */dev/rfd0135ds18*
Formats a 1.44 Mbyte 3.5" floppy placed in the first floppy drive.

See also:
dosformat; fdformat.

ftp
transferring files with file transfer protocol

The tool most often used to transfer data on a TCP/IP network is **ftp** (file transfer protocol).

Command:
ftp [**-v**] [**-d**] [**-i**] [**-n**] [**-t**] [**-i**] [*host*]

Function:
File transfer between two computers using TCP/IP.

Options:

-v	(verbose). Forces **ftp** to display all responses and file transfer statistics.
-d	Enables debugging.
-i	Turns off prompts during multiple file transfers.
-n	Stops **ftp** from attempting automatic login on the ***host***.
-t	Enables packet tracing.
-g	Disables file globbing.

Arguments:

host	Name of the remote host with which **ftp** is to communicate

NOTE:
To transfer binary files you must specify **binary** at the `ftp>` prompt. For example:

```
ftp> binary
```

Examples:

ftp is an interactive program. If you do not specify a *host*, your prompt is changed to `ftp>`. From this prompt you may choose to give several commands, for example,

`ftp>`**help**
Displays **ftp** commands.

`ftp>`**open scsserver**
Connects to the computer specified by **scsserver**.

`ftp>`**close**
Terminates an ftp session.

To move around the host computer's directory structure, you can use commands like **cd** (**lcd** changes the directory on the local system), **pwd**, **ls** and **dir**.
To import a file from a remote computer, use **get** and the filename. For example:
`ftp>`**get** *datafile*

To export a file to a remote computer, use **put** and the filename. For example:
`ftp>`**put** *data file*

To copy several files at once use **mput** (multiple put) and **mget** (multiple get). **ftp** recognizes the wildcards * and ?. Thus, the commands:
mput *chap.**
and
mget *chap.**

would put or get all files named *chap.* with any extension.

See also:

ftp; ping; rcp; rlogin; rsh (rcmd); telnet.

grep, egrep and fgrep
finding data or text in UNIX files

With help of **grep** (global regular expression print), you can find character patterns in files and directories. If you do not redirect the output, the result of any given **grep** is displayed on the screen.

grep is a family of commands, including **grep, fgrep** and **egrep**. Each of them has its advantages and disadvantages. **grep** uses less memory than **egrep**, but is usually slower. **fgrep**, meaning fixed grep, finds defined strings of characters. **egrep**, meaning extended grep, is a more advanced program that accepts more complex expressions.

Command:
grep [- vciln] *expression* [*file* ...]

Function:
Searches a file (or files) for a regular expression (or text pattern).

Options:

- c	Displays a count of the number of lines containing the text string.
- i	Ignores case distinctions (uppercase and lowercase).
- l	Prints the names of files containing matching lines.
- n	Displays all line numbers and lines that match search pattern.
- v	Displays all lines that do not match the search pattern.

Arguments:

expression	String or expression sought.
files	Files to search (with or without the wildcards, *, ?, [ ]).

Without options, and with only one text string and one filename specified, **grep** finds and displays all lines containing the text string. Note that if a string has several words, it must be set off with quotations.

With **egrep**, you can use the following additional expressions:

textstring +secondstring+...   Searches for *textstring* plus one or more *second-strings.*

textstring ?   Searches for *textstring* plus one character.

expression1 | expression2   Searches for either *expression1* or *expression2.*

Examples:

grep examples:
grep david *datafile*
Displays all lines in *datafile* containing the word david on the screen.

grep - n Peter *datafile*
Displays the line numbers containing the text string Peter in *datafile.*

grep - c Peter *datafile*
Displays a count of the number of lines in *datafile* containing the pattern Peter.

grep - v Peter *datafile*
Displays all lines that do not contain the pattern Peter in *datafile.*

grep - i Peter *datafile*
Displays all lines containing the text string peter in *datafile.* The -i option specifies that **grep** ignore the case of the string.

grep - l ansi */etc/termcap /etc/termcap.old /usr/lib/terminfo/a/ansi*
Displays the name of any of the files specified that contain the string ansi.

grep - n set *
Searches all files in the current working directory for the text string set. All lines containing set found by **grep** are displayed with line numbers.

If you search for the special characters [,], }, {, \, | and $, you can turn off their special function with a ' (quotation character) on each side of the special characters. For example, the command
grep - n '\|' *
searches all files for the string enclosed in quotation marks (\|). All lines containing the string are displayed with line numbers.

grep 'Philip' *letter.doc*
Displays lines containing the text string Philip in *letter.doc*.

grep 'O..' *letter.doc*
Displays all lines with words of 3 characters, where the first character is O in *letter.doc* .

grep '[Pp]hilip' *letter.doc*
Displays all lines containing Philip or philip in *letter.doc*.

grep '[^o- z]le' *letter.doc*
Displays all lines containing 3 character words that do not begin with the letters o to z and that end with the letters le.

grep ',$' *letter.doc*
Displays all lines ending with a comma (,) in *letter.doc*.

grep - n '^$' *letter.doc*
Displays the line number on all empty lines in *letter.doc*.

fgrep example:
fgrep "david" *word.doc*
Searches for the text string david in *word.doc*. **fgrep** specifies a fixed text string.

egrep examples:
egrep 'An+e' *namelist*
In *namelist*, searches for the text string Ane, Anne, Anmme, etc.

egrep 'david | dave' *namelist*
In *namelist*, searches for the text strings david or dave.

egrep "([0-9] + USA)* DE" *database*
In the file *database*, searches for strings that begin with one or more digits, followed by the text USA, and with any ending. The search ends when **egrep** finds the string DE.

Internet communication
UNIX networking

Networking means connecting your computers (often called network nodes or hosts) together so that you can communicate with other users and share information either by mail or by making files and filesystems available to other network users. Effective networking increases productivity and is a relatively easy way to more efficiently distribute resources to those that most need them.

Internet (or *the internet*) is an expression that refers to a world-wide system of networks and network connections. While other protocols are used on the internet, TCP/IP (Transmission Control Protocol/Internet Protocol) is the most common network protocol, providing the basic set of rules or protocols by which computers on the internet communicate with each other. These protocols describe how to format and pass messages from computer to computer as well as how to check for and handle errors in transmission. By defining these types of functions, these protocols allow many different types of computers to communicate with each other. Many large networks subscribe to the TCP/IP protocols, including DARPA (Defense Advanced Research Projects Agency) Internet, BITNET, and CSNET.

The TCP/IP protocols

Protocols are really "protocol suites" or "protocol families". This grouping reflects the fact that network communication is so complex that it must be divided into independent layers or levels. Each layer only passes information to the layers immediately above and below it. The lower levels are closer to the host hardware, the higher levels are closer to the user. The number of layers and tasks is defined by the protocol family. For example, in addition to Transmission Control Protocol and Internet Protocol, TCP/IP consists of a whole family of service protocols and commands, most of which are listed in the following table. The RFC number refers to the Request For Comment number. To obtain copies of an RFC, contact the **Network Information Center, Suite 200, 14200 Park Meadow Drive, Chantilly, VA. 22021.**

TCP	Transmission Control Protocol	(RFC793)
UDP	User Datagram Protocol	(RFC768)
IP	Internet Protocol	(RFC791)
ARP	Address Resolution Protocol	(RFC826)
ICMP	Internet Control Message Protocol	(RFC792)

SMTP   Simple Mail Transport Protocol
RIP   Routing Information Protocol
SLIP   Serial Line Internet Protocol

System files in a UNIX-based TCP/IP network

If your system is not running the BIND (Berkeley Internet Name Domain) server, the most important system files for a TCP/IP network are */etc/hosts*, */etc/hosts.equiv* and *$HOME/.rhosts*. (The BIND server provides a distributed lookup service for host names and addresses for large networks. On large networks, using BIND means that system administrators no longer have to maintain large numbers of network system files on a multitude of host machines.)

On systems not using the BIND server, */etc/hosts* provides TCP/IP computers with a list of hosts that share a network. */etc/hosts* is used by programs that need to translate between host names (e.g., **danton@sco.com**) and Internet addresses (e.g.,132.147.24.103). If a host name is listed in */etc/hosts*, programs can use that name instead of the more difficult-to-remember Internet address.

/etc/hosts.equiv contains the list of what are known as "trusted hosts". Quite simply, a trusted host is a machine whose users you trust. If a TCP/IP remote command (e.g., **rlogin**, **rcmd** or **rsh**) is issued from a trusted host by a user whose user ID is found in the local host's */etc/passwd* file, the command is executed without qualification.

The *$HOME/.rhosts* file functions in much the same way as */etc/hosts.equiv* If a remote host is placed in a local user's *.rhost* file, all users from the remote host can log in (and execute files) on the local user's account. The file has two columns. The first column lists the host computer name, the second lists the name of the user able to login without a password.

See also:

ftp; ping; rcp; rlogin; rsh; telnet.

Kernel
The UNIX kernel

UNIX is a large program subdivided into several larger and smaller programs. The most important part of UNIX is the kernel. The UNIX kernel is loaded into memory at system start-up and remains in memory to manage system resources. Most other parts of the UNIX operating system do not remain in memory. The kernel ensures that these parts are fetched from the hard disk to memory when needed. The kernel is an *a.out* file which is similar to a compiled C program. It contains all the drivers for installed devices (e.g., floppy disks) as well as other system information.

You communicate with the UNIX kernel via programs called shells.

See also:
Bourne shell; C-shell; Korn shell; App. A-about shell scripts.

kill
stopping UNIX processes

Although there are many ways to stop UNIX processes, the most commonly used are the terminal's interrupt key, (<**Del**>) and the **kill** command.

The terminal interrupt key (<**Del**>) can only stop processes running in the foreground. If a UNIX process is running in the background, you must know the process identification number (PID) and you must use **kill**. While users may **kill** any process they own, only the system administrator may stop processes owned by other users.

Command:
kill [*signal number*] [**process ID number**]

Function:
Stops a UNIX process.

Arguments:

signal number   Level of **kill** signal. This number is dependent on the type of UNIX and multiprocessor found on the system. This is one example:

1	hang up
2	interrupt
3	quit
4	illegal instruction
5	trace trap
6	IOT instruction
7	EMT instruction
8	floating point exception
9	kill
10	bus error
11	segmentation violation
12	bad argument to system call
13	write on a pipe with no one to read it
14	alarm clock
15	soft kill

16	user defined signal 1
17	death of a child
19	power-fail restart

On SVR4 systems the command **kill -l** lists the symbolic signal names.

process ID number   (PID). Identification number of the process. Use
ps -fu *username*
to determine the PID numbers belonging to all the processes belonging to *username*.

Examples:

Solaris:
If you issue the command
kill -l
you see output resembling the following:

```
HUP    INT   QUIT  ILL   TRAP  ABRT  EMT   FPE     KILL BUS
SEGV   SYS   PIPE  ALRM  TERM  USR1  USR2  CLD     PWR  WINCH
RUG    POLL  STOP  TSTP  CONT  TTIN  TTOU  VTALRM  PROF XCPU
XFSZ   WAITING     LWP
```

UnixWare:
If you issue the command
kill -l
you see output resembling the following:

```
HUP    INT   QUIT  ILL   TRAP  ABRT  EMT   FPE     KILL  BUS
SEGV   SYS   PIPE  ALRM  TERM  USR1  USR2  CLD     PWR   WINCH
URG    POLL  STOP  TSTP  CONT  TTIN  TTOU  VTALRM  PROF  XCPU
XFSZ
```

Killing processes

In many cases, it is necessary to terminate a process. For example, you may need to terminate a background process that never finishes. The most usual situation, however, is when you "hang up" a terminal. When a terminal hangs up, it cannot be freed or released. When you hang your terminal, you must kill the process that spawned it.

If you have a hung terminal, you can log yourself on to another terminal and enter **ps**. If you know the terminal number of the hanging terminal, you can enter the following command, where tty03 is the number of the hung terminal. The following example shows the command and the output

ps -t *tty03*

```
PID TTY         TIME COMMAND
399  03        0:02 du
342  03        0:01 csh
400  03        0:00 grep
```

If you do not know the terminal name, you can enter:
ps -ft *console*

or you can get a full status by entering
ps -ef
Both of these variants will give you the process ID for the hanging process. Then, you can stop the process with the **kill** command. For example, if the hung process has a PID of 400 the command
kill -9 400
terminates it.

If you are unsure of the PID for a hung process, you can terminate the user's shell that spawned it. Still using the output from the **ps** command above, the command
kill -9 342
terminates the user's C-shell (PID 342). If you do this, the user has to login again.

Other examples

kill -15 789
Kills process 789 with signal number 15. If signal number 15 does not work, try signal number 9.

kill -0
Kills all the background jobs (SCO UNIX only).

kill -1 1
The system administrator sets the system to single-user mode (SCO only).

See also:
processes; ps.

Korn shell
Configuring your work environment

As an alternative to Bourne shell and C-shell, Dave Korn wrote Korn shell (**ksh**). The Korn shell is compatible with the Bourne shell, but contains additional components that make it superior in some ways to C- shell in its interactive capabilities. Korn shell is very efficient and is becoming the next "standard" UNIX shell.

If you use the Korn shell, you define your working environment with the system file *.profile.* The *.profile* file is executed each time you login to the system.

Commands that are only understood by **ksh** are defined in a user's *$HOME/.kshrc*. If set, *.kshrc* is read each time you start a **ksh**. If you want to use this file to set up your **ksh** environment, set the **ENV** environment variable in your *.profile* to point to *.kshrc*. You can do this by adding the following line to your *.profile.*

```
ENV=$HOME/.kshrc
export ENV
```

To exit the Korn shell, enter **<Ctrl-d>** or **exit** at the shell prompt.

Important Korn shell options and environment variables

The following is a list, together with a short explanation of the most important **ksh** options and variables. You can define environment variables in your *.profile* or (if you have set it up) *.kshrc* file.

set   Options are examined and changed with the **set** command. Korn shell has many options you can set with the **set** command. Many are similar to those found in Bourne and C-shell (See Bourne shell and C-shell). Among other things, **set** is used to assign arguments to shell environment parameters and display the names and values of the currently defined shell environment variables. Below are a few examples of **set,** together with a description of what each does.

set	Displays the currently defined options and environment variables.
set -v	Causes **ksh** to display each command in a shell script as it is read.
set -m	Instructs **ksh** to inform the user when each background job is finished.
set -n	Reads but does not execute commands in shell scripts. This function is used to check shell scripts for errors.

For example, **set** with no options produces output resembling the following:

```
CODEPAGE=pc437
COUNTRY=1
ERRNO=25
FCEDIT=/bin/ed
HOME=/home/vigdis
HZ=100
IFS=
KEYB=us
LANG=no
LINENO=1
LOGNAME=vigdis
LOGTTY=/dev/console
MAIL=/var/mail/vigdis
MAILCHECK=600
OPTARG
OPTIND=1
PATH=/usr/bin:/usr/dbin:/usr/ldbin:/usr/c/bin
PPID=1
PS1=$
PS2=>
PS3=#?
PS4=+
PWD=/home/vigdis
RANDOM=31610
SECONDS=70
SHELL=/usr/bin/ksh
```

```
TERM=AT386-ie
TERMCAP=/etc/termcap
TIMEOUT=0
TMOUT=0
TZ=:CET
XKEYBOARD=NO
XMODIFIERS=@im=Local
XNLSPATH=/usr/X/lib/nls/elsXsi
_=-la
```

unset   Use the unset command to remove a variable. The syntax is
                 unset *variablename*
                 where ***variablename*** is the name of the variable you want to un-
                 set. This is the same as in C-shell.

HISTSIZE   Defines the size of the history list. Every time you enter a com-
                 mand for execution, **ksh** stores each command in a history list.
                 All the commands are numbered in sequence. The default size of
                 HISTSIZE is 128 commands. To change **HISTSIZE** to 200, is-
                 sue the following command:
                 HISTSIZE=200
                 export HISTSIZE
                 These command tell **ksh** to remember the 200 most recent com-
                 mands in the history list. To clear the history list, remove
                 $HOME/.sh_history (default name of the history file).

HISTFILE   Sets the name of the history list file. By default, as you enter
                 command lines for execution, the Korn shell stores each com-
                 mand in *$HOME/.sh_history*. You can tell **ksh** to use a different
                 file with the following commands:
                 HISTFILE=*/usr/david/.historyfile*
                 export $HISTFILE
                 If you have defined the HISTSIZE environment variable, you can
                 access the history list by using command editing features. Korn
                 shell treats the history list as an editable file. By default, at the
                 ksh prompt, the system is in input mode in the history list file.
                 Every line you type is added to the end of the file when you press
                 <Enter>.

If you have defined the environment variable **VISUAL=vi,** to edit previous commands press **<Esc>**. This starts the command mode of a **vi**-style editor. You can now use common **vi** commands such as h, l, j, k etc. To modify text, use the **vi** insert commands **i** or **a**, add some text, and then use **<Esc>** to return to command mode. When you press **<Enter>**, **ksh** assumes you have finished editing. The **vi ex** commands (the commands the begin with a colon ":") do not work. However, you can use many of the move commands and search operators to retrieve and edit commands from the history list.

VISUAL   Name of the type of editor to use in **ksh**. In **ksh**, you define the style of editor you use for **ksh** functions. To select a **vi** style editor enter
  VISUAL=vi
  export VISUAL
To select an **emacs** style editor, enter
  VISUAL=emacs
  export VISUAL

alias/unalias   Creates and removes as many aliases as you wish. To create a alias, use the alias command, as shown here:
  alias dir="ls -la"
Once this alias is set, **ksh** replaces **dir** with its alias (**ls -la**) whenever it is used on the command line. Users with DOS experience configure aliases so that if they inadvertently enter DOS commands, they are translated into their UNIX equivalents.

You remove a previously established alias with **unalias**. For example,
  unalias dir
removes the alias we created above.

whence   Locate the exact form of the command you specify. You use **whence** to find the location of a given command or to expand an aliased command. For normal commands, **whence** will give you the full path name. If the command is a built-in or shell function, **ksh** gives the name without a path. If the command is aliased, **whence** translates the alias into what is actually executed.

For example, the command
whence ksh
produces the output
`/usr/bin/ksh`

The command
whence dir
produces the output:
`ls -la`

fc Selects and then executes a range of commands from the history list. With **fc** you can select a range of commands from the history list (*$HOME/.sh_history*), edit this range with your editor, and then execute the edited commands.

For example, the command
fc -l
displays the contents of the history list.

The following command starts your editor with commands 10-16, one per line:
fc 10 16
When you quit the editor, the commands will be executed.

FCEDIT **fc** can be set to use any editor you choose by setting the **FCEDIT** environment variable. To set **FCEDIT** to be **vi,** use the following commands:
FCEDIT=vi
export FCEDIT

Or, to use any other editor, use the commands
FCEDIT=$*EDITORNAME*
export FCEDIT
where ***EDITORNAME*** is the editor of your choice.

PS1 Defines your prompt. The default value for the prompt is the $ character. For example, the line
PS1=Give command:
defines the prompt to be the text "`Give command`".

PS2   Secondary prompt. You see this prompt when your shell expects more input. By default, **PS2** is set to >. For example, the line
PS2=+
defines the secondary prompt to be the character, "+"(plus).

IFS   Defines which variable is used as field separator. Internal field separators usually are space, tab and new line. For example,
IPS=,
defines the , (comma) as the field separator.

pwd   Prints your current working directory. For example,
pwd
`/u/laurad`

CDPATH   Specifies the search path for the **cd** command. Once this path is set the shell interpreter uses the directories named in **CDPATH** as working directories for the **cd** command. For example, if you issue the commands
CDPATH=*/w/unix/man:/w/unix/X:/w/unix/tcp*
export CDPATH
then each time you use **cd** to change directories, **cd** treats */w/unix/man, /w/unix/X* and */w/unix/tcp* as current working directories.

See also:
Bourne shell; C-shell; App. A- about shell scripts.

ksh
invoking the Korn shell command interpreter

ksh is a command interpreter. It (like the Bourne and C-shells) helps the user to control the operating system kernel. Unlike the Bourne shell, **ksh** is a more flexible interactive command interpreter. Unlike C-shell, **ksh** uses a Bourne shell like syntax. If your login shell is Korn shell your **ksh** UNIX session begins by executing commands in your *.profile* and (if you set it up) *.kshrc* files. Typing **ksh** at any UNIX command line automatically starts a Korn shell (a subshell).

See also:
Bourne shell; C-shell; Korn shell.

ln
linking files

Sometimes it's useful to link files together. Doing so allows you to make use of several names for a single file. One of the names may show which project the file belongs to, while another could tell something about the content of the file. **ln** is the command used to link files.. **ln** links two filenames to the same inode number.

The **-s** option is used to symbolically link files from different file systems.

Command:
ln [-fs] *file1 file2*
or
ln [-fs] *file1 ... directory*

Function:
Creates a link to a file, i.e., makes it possible to use several names for one file. The file named *file1* also gets the name *file2*

Options:

-f   Forces creation of the link, even if it means overwriting an existing file or changing access permissions.

-s   Creates a symbolic link or links. A symbolic link allows you to link files across filesystems.

A regular (or hard) link links an existing file to a new filename. The new filename is a standard directory entry just like the original. Hard links can be made to different directories but cannot be made across file systems.

A symbolic link (**-s** option) link creates a special directory entry that points to another file. Symbolic links can span filesystems and point to directories. You can create a symbolic link linking a filename to a file that is not present in the current file system.

Some systems link **mv**, **cp**, **ln** and **ls** (and **ex**, **vi**, **e**, **edit** and **view**) to the same program. Each linked program executes a slightly different version of the binary.

Note that to create a file link, you must have write permission in the new file-name's directory. Thus, for the following command to work, you must have write permission in *usr/laurad*:

ln */usr/kentd/.profile /usr/laurad/.profile*

Examples:

ln *project.B source.c*
Links files *project.B* and *source.c*.

ln *.login /usr/anne/.login*
Links one user's *.login* file to */usr/anne/.login*. The link goes across directories.

ln */dev/rfd096ds15 /dev/rfd0*
Device drivers sometimes have long names. This command links the device driver for a 5.25" 1.2 Mbyte floppy drive (*/dev/rfd096ds*) to the much simpler filename */dev/rfd0*. Note that because you are creating a file in the *dev* directory, to link device files you must be *root*.

ln -s */usr/flib/books/man /home/share/man*
Makes a symbolic link between the directories on two different filesystems (*/usr/flib/books/man* and */home/share/man*).

Both hard- and symbolically-linked files are removed in the same manner as any other file (i.e., with rm). For example,
rm *project.B*
removes the linked filename *project.B* and removes the link.

See also:
cp; rm; mv.

lp
printing UNIX files

Use **lp** to print files. **lp** causes files to be placed in the UNIX print queue. The UNIX print scheduler then directs files to printers and returns a print-request job id number. If there are several printers on the system, you can use the **-d** option to select a printer. If no specific printer is chosen, the default printer is used.

Command:
lp [-wcnso] [-d*printer*] [*argument*]

Function:
Sends a print request to a printer.

Options:

-w   Writes the user's terminal when the print job is finished.

-c   Copies the file before printing. Normally, files will not be copied, but will be linked whenever possible. If the **-c** option is not specified, then you should be careful not to remove any of the files before the request has been printed in its entirety.

-d*printer*   Sends the file to the printer specified by ***printer***

-n*x*   Tells **lp** that you want x number of copies of the output

-s   Suppresses messages from **lp** such as "request id is ...."

-o*option*   Specifies local system, printer and class dependent options. Several printer-specific parameters may be specified. Refer to your UNIX user's reference for more information on your systems local options. Some of the standard options are as follows:

             cpi   Specifies characters per inch. **-o** can also take **pica** or **elite** as options, specifying 10 or 12 characters per inch, respectively.

length=*n*	*n* specifies page length. Can be set in centimeters (**length=*n*c),** inches (*n***i**), or lines (*n*).
nobanner	Specifies that no banner page be printed. A banner is a cover page that includes login ID, time, name of the printer, name of the print-job etc.
nofilebreak	Stops formfeed between files
stty=*options*	Causes **lp** to use *options* for the **stty** command
width=*n*	Set the page width. Can be set in centimeters (**length=*n*c),** inches (*n***i**), or characters (*n*).

Arguments:

argument	One (or more) files to be printed.

Under SCO UNIX, Solaris and UnixWare you can use **lp** (System V) or **lpr** (BSD).

Examples:

lp *letter1 letter2 letter3*
Sends the files *letter1*, *letter2* and *letter3* to the default printer.

lp -dprinter2 *.cshrc*
Sends the file *.cshrc* to the printer named printer2.

lp -dprinter1 -n 4 *offer*
Sends 4 copies of *offer* to the printer named printer1.

---

lp -c *datafile*
Makes a copy of the file *datafile* and sends it to the default printer.

lp -printer1 -w *datafile*
Sends the file *datafile* to the printer named printer1. When printing is complete, **lp** writes a message to that effect directly to the screen.

lp -o "length=72, width=80, nobanner" *letter*
Sends *letter* to the default printer, specifying a page length of 72 lines, a page width of 80 characters and no banner page.

Files:
/etc/lp*, /var/spool/lp/*, /usr/spool/lp/* (SCO).

See also:
cancel; lpstat; Print spooling.

lpstat
determining line printer status

lpstat provides many kinds of information about print jobs and services. **lpstat** is available both to the system administrator and to individual users.

Command:

lpstat [*options*] [*request-ID-list*]

Function:

Print information about status of the **lp** print service.

Options:

-o [*list*] [*-l*]   Reports on the status of print requests. It has the following options:

        list   A list of intermixed printer names, class names, and request-IDs. The keyletter **-o** may be omitted.

        -l   A longer list of print details about *list*. For example, for each print request, the **-l** option causes **lpstat** to display whether it is assigned to or being printed on a printer, the form required (if any), and the character set or print wheel required (if any).

-d   Displays the name of the default printer (if any) on the system.

-p [*list*] [*-D*] [*-l*]   If **-D** option is specified, a brief description is printed for each printer in *list*. If the **-l** option is specified, a full description of each printer's configuration is given, including the form mounted, printer types, etc.

-r   Displays print scheduler status (i.e., running or not running).The print scheduler is called **lpsched**.

-t Displays information of the status of all printers in the UNIX system.

-u [*user* ...] Displays the status of jobs initiated from *user*.

Examples:

lpstat apl5
Displays the status of the printer named apl5.

Use the following command to display the status of the whole print spooling system:

lpstat -t
Displays output resembling the following:

```
Scheduler is running
no system default destination
members of class class:
     printer
device for printer: /dev/lp1
class not accepting requests since Fri Oct  5 14:17:42 1990-
     new destination
printer accepting requests since Fri Oct  5 14:19:08 1990
printer printer is idle.
enabled since Fri Oct  5 14:19:17
1990. available.
```

lpstat -d
Displays the system default print destination. For example,

```
system default destination: brother
```

If you do not specify any printer when using **lp**, the print job is sent to the default printer.

lpstat -o
Displays the status of all print requests.

lpstat -r
Causes **lpstat** to check and report on the status of the print scheduler. For example,

```
scheduler is running
```

lpstat -u david
Shows the status of all of user david's print jobs. For example,

```
oki400-2      david   692 Oct 17 17:53 on oki400
oki400-3      david    34 ag 16 October
oki400-2      david    50 ag 16 October
```

lpstat -p -D
Displays output resembling the following.

```
printer gans is idle.
enabled since Mon Aug 16 14:58:26 1993. available.
Description: Hegel's wonderful note taker
printer doslp is idle.
enabled since Fri Aug 20 05:54:51 1993. available.
Description:
printer Citizen is idle.
enabled since Fri Dec 31 09:27:35 1993. available.
Description: Citizen MSP 10
```

Files:
/etc/lp*; */var/spool/lp/**; */usr/spool/lp/** (SCO)

See also:
cancel; lp; Print spooling.

ls
listing files

ls and the **ls** family of commands (e.g., **l, lc, lf** and **lr**) display a list of files. **ls** is the UNIX equivalent to the DOS **DIR** command.

Command:
ls [-aCilrRt] [*directory*]

Function:
Lists the content of specified directory. By default, **ls** produces an alphabetical list of the files in the current working directory. By using different options, you can include different information in the list, such as owner, group and size (number of characters or bytes) etc.

Options:

-a   Shows all files including system files (those starting with a dot), e.g., *profile, .login, .cshrc, .mailrc* etc.

-C   Displays the files and directories in column format

-i   Displays inode numbers.

-l   Displays in long format. The complete format gives:
  • permissions
  • number of links
  • owner
  • size
  • date

-r   Sorts in reverse order.

-R   Displays contents of all directories recursively.

-t   Displays files in chronological order.

There are more options than this. Use the command **man ls** to see the full listing for your system. **ls** with no options displays all regular files and directories in the current working directory. It lists only the names of the files and directories. System files (those prefixed by a dot) are not included in the list. To see the system files use the **-a** option.

Arguments:

directory   Any filename or directory. With no argument **ls** displays the contents of the current working directory.

Examples:

ls -la
Displays a list of all files and directories, including those that begin with a dot (system files). The list is displayed in long format.

ls -lt
Displays all files (except those that begin with a dot) and directories in chronological order in the current working directory.

Try the UNIX commands **lc** and **lf**. They are variations on the command **ls,** but they use different default settings.

See also:
chmod; find.

mail
electronic mail

UNIX electronic mail or "email" is a powerful communication system making it possible for the UNIX user to do the following:

- create mail
- send mail
- receive mail
- forward mail to others
- reply to previous mail

You can send electronic mail to one user or to several users at a time. You can send mail even if the addressee isn't logged on. All mail is stored in each user's electronic mailbox file. When he or she logs in, UNIX displays a "mail waiting" message.

If your system is part of a Local Area Network (LAN) or Wide Area Network (WAN), you can send and receive mail for all users and machines that are part of your network. If you are part of the Internet, you can reach electronic mail users from all over the world.

When you address electronic mail to a given user, **mail** first determines which computer the letter should be sent to, then attempts to send it. Once sent, **mail** checks to ensure the target computer actually received the letter.

Among many others, UNIX electronic mail can use the following network systems for transport:

- Micnet (only SCO UNIX/Xenix)
- UUCP (UNIX to UNIX copy)
- TCP/IP (Simple Mail Transfer Protocol)

UNIX has many electronic mail systems. The most common are **mailx** and **Mail**. These two systems are almost identical. **mailx** is the name of the electronic mail system on UNIX system V and **Mail** on Berkeley UNIX (BSD) systems. Some systems are set up with an "alias" so that when you type **mail** the **mailx** (UNIX System V) or **Mail** (BSD UNIX) is run. To keep things simple, we refer to all systems as **mail**. Nonetheless, the options on your system may vary from those described below. Refer to your User's Reference for more information.

Command:

mail [*options*] [*mailaddress*]

Function:

If no options or mail addresses are specified, **mail** reads the user's electronic mailbox: otherwise, **mail** behaves as defined below.

Options:

-u *user*　　If you have read permission on the mailbox file, opens the mailbox of the user specified by *user*. If you use the **-u** option, you must specify a username as an argument.

-f *mailfile*　　Opens *mailfile* instead of the user's mailbox. If you use the **-f** option, must specify the name of a mail file.

-s *subject*　　Specifies the subject of outgoing mail. If you use the **-s** option you must also specify a subject of the outgoing mail.

If you invoke **mail** with no options, it opens your electronic mailbox.

Arguments:

mailaddress　　A username, an alias, or a username and network address. For example, the following command sends mail to markt on the local system or network:

　　mail markt

Similarly, the following command sends mail to a user at a different network address:

　　mail gwfhegel@sco.com

mailaddress may also be a mail "alias". For example, you could send mail to the following alias:

　　mail aardvarks

where **aardvarks** is an alias for a group of users.

For more information about defining and using mail aliases, see the section entitled "Mail aliases and the *.mailrc* file" below.

Sending local electronic mail

To send electronic mail to a user on your system, you need only specify the addressees username. (Usually, this is also the case for users on the same LAN.)

mail john
Starts a letter to user **john**. By default, **mail** then prompts for a subject. Give a short description of the message (e.g., lunch-meeting, project, seminar, etc.). After specifying the subject press **<Enter>** and compose the letter. When you finish, press **<Ctrl>d**, (or dot "." on some UNIX systems) to end the letter and send the mail (letter).

mail philip else anne
Starts a letter that will be sent to three users at the same time.

You may also mail files written with other word processing systems or editors . For example, the following command mails the file *letter.offer* to user **mary.**
mail mary < *letter.offer*

You may skip the subject prompt by specifying the **mail** subject on the UNIX command line. For example,
mail -s "Important meeting" peter nicholas jessica<*report*
This command sends the file *report* to users **peter**, **nicholas** and **jessica** under the subject heading, Important meeting.

Receiving electronic mail

The first time you log in to a new system, you receive mail from the operating system (usually *root*). For example,
```
You have mail!
```

If you receive mail after you log in, **mail** prompts you with a message resembling the following:

```
You have new mail
```

After logging in, try using mail by entering **mail.** After starting up **mail** lists all the electronic mail you have received. Different UNIX systems display your mail differently. Below are examples from SCO UNIX, UnixWare and Solaris.

SCO UNIX:
```
SCO System V Mail (version 3.2)  Type ? for help.
"/usr/spool/mail/david": 2 messages 2 new
 N  2 root              Sat Jul  6 01:51   10/290   project-1
>N  1 philip            Sat Jul  6 01:47   10/251   lunch
```

For help with **mail** commands, press <?>. **mail** displays the following information:

```
&?
                        mailx commands
type [msglist]          print messages
next                    goto and type next message
edit [msglist]          edit messages
from [msglist]          give header lines of messages
delete [msglist]        delete messages
undelete [msglist]      restore deleted messages
save [msglist] file     append messages to file
reply [msglist]         reply to the authors of the messages
Reply [message]         reply to message, including all recipi-
                        ents
preserve [msglist]      preserve messages in mailbox
mail user               mail to specific user
quit                    quit, preserving unread messages
exit                    quit, preserving all messages
header                  print page of active message headers
!                       shell escape
cd [directory]          chdir to directory or home if none given
list                    list all commands (no explanations)
top [msglist]           print top 5 lines of messages
z [-]                   display next [last] page of 10 headers

[msglist] is optional and specifies messages by number,
author, subject or type.  The default is the current message.
```

mail

Solaris/UnixWare:
```
mailx version 4.2 (UnixWare) Type ? for help.
"/var/mail/david": 1 message 1 unread
>U  1 lp                   Sat Feb  6 22:08     20/596    Problem
? Held 1 message in /var/mail/david
```

For help with Solaris and UnixWare mail commands, press <?>

```
? ?          print this help message
#            display message number #
-            print previous
+            next (no delete)
! cmd        execute cmd
<CR>         next (no delete)
a            position at and read newly arrived mail
d [#]        delete message # (default current message)
dp           delete current message and print the next
dq           delete current message and exit
h a          display all headers
h d          display headers of letters scheduled for deletion
h [#]        display headers around # (default current message)
m user       mail (and delete) current message to user
M user       mail (and delete) current message to user, with
             comments
n            next (no delete)
p            print (override any warnings of binary content)
P            override default 'brief' mode and display ALL
             header   lines
q, ^D        quit
r [args]     reply to (and delete) current letter via mail
             [args]
R [args]     reply to (and delete) current letter via mail
             [args],  including message
s [files]    save (and delete) current message (default mbox)
u [#]        undelete message # (default current message)
w [files]    save (and delete) current message without header
x            exit without changing mail
y [files]    save (and delete) current message (default mbox)
```

Press **n** (on all systems) to see the first message. If you press **n** again, you will see the next message, and so on.

The following are examples of commands issued from the **mail** prompt.
1
Displays message number 1.

-
Displays the previous message.

l
Sends the current letter to the default printer (SCO).

p
Sends the current letter to the default printer (Solaris and UnixWare)

mail lorim
Begins a mail message to user lorim (SCO).

d
Delete current message.

u
Restores (undeletes) previously deleted message.

r
Replies to the originator of current mail message.

s *mail.list*
Saves current message to file *mail.list*.

h
Prints list of active message headers.

You can also execute shell commands from the mail prompt. To issue a shell command, prefix the command with an exclamation point (!). For example,
!date
This starts a command shell and then issues the command **date**. After executing the command the shell returns the mail prompt.

!uniplex
Does the same as the previous example, except that the command shell runs the command **uniplex**.

If you receive new mail while you are in **mail** program, you see a message resembling the following:
```
New mail has arrived -- type 'restart' to read
```

To read the new mail, enter:
restart

q
Quits the mail program, preserving all unread messages.

Sending external mail
If you send mail to users on other remote systems, you must add the system name to the user name. If the addressee is on the internet the usual format for the address is the following:
user@computername
so, to send mail to **user@computername** you would enter
mail user@computername

If your network is based on Micnet or uucp, instead of the symbol @, the separator is usually : or !. So, on a Micnet network the full **mail** command would resemble the following:
mail user:computername

and a uucp network mail command would be:
mail user!computername

On some uucp networks the syntax may be reversed. So instead of the above, you may have to enter the following:
mail computername!user
or
mail computername:user

Micnet network examples (SCO UNIX):

If your computer is connected to a Micnet network, specify user name and computer name separated by a colon. In this case, you specify the computer or system name and the user name. For example,

mail Support:david
Begins a letter to user **david** whose home account is on the computer **Support**.

mail Courseroom:philip sale:peter
Begins a letter to **philip** whose home account is on the computer **Courseroom** and to **peter** whose home account is on the computer **sale.**

uucp networks (All systems):

You may also send mail to computers connected via a uucp (UNIX-to-UNIX copy) network. The syntax for uucp networks is **computername!username**. For example,

mail Support!david
The exclamation point indicates the attempt to access an external computer. **Support** is the name of the computer and **david** is the user name.

It is also possible to route mail to a computer via another computer. For example,
mail Oslo!Support!david
The mail is first sent to the computer **Oslo** and then further on to **Support**. A configuration-file on **Oslo**, updated by the system administrator, locates the external system.

NOTE:

If you are using a C-shell, you must escape the exclamation marks (!). For example:

mail Oslo\!Support\!david

Mail aliases and the .mailrc file

If you have a global mail system, it can be a lot of work to specify long addresses for mailing. Similarly, it can be difficult to send the same mail to a large group of people. A *.mailrc* file can help with both tasks.

Group definitions

You can create aliases if you wish to mail to several users, to groups of users, or to users on other UNIX systems. The definitions are set up in your *.mailrc* file. This file is placed in your home directory and is read every time you start **mail.** The following is an example of a *.mailrc* file:

Sample *.mailrc* **file:**

```
alias infogroup anne david peter jane
alias proj david peter Support:rita Support:eve Croom:demo
alias department Chicago!jessica Jeremy!lesley
alias emaildep doris@Server1 anne@Server2 per@Central
```

If this were your *.mailrc* file and you issue the command
mail infogroup
you would begin a letter to the mail alias **infogroup**, which includes the users anne, david, peter and jane. Similarly, when you send mail to the alias **proj**, the message is sent to david and peter on your local network; to rita and eve at the computer Support and user demo at the computer Croom. These systems are connected to the local system via a Micnet or a Xenix-net network.

If you send mail to the mail alias **department**, the message is sent to the computers Chicago and Jeremy. The users receiving mail are jessica and lesley. If you send mail to the last alias **emaildep**, mail is sent on the internet to the users **doris@Server1**, **anne@Server2** and **per@Central.** The names before the @ are usernames, the names after the @ are system or computer names.

Configuring your mail environment with *.mailrc*

To configure your mail environment, use the **set** command in your *.mailrc* file.
To see a list of mail configuration parameters, enter **set** or **?** from your mail
prompt. You see a list resembling the following:

```
DEAD="/usr/david/dead.letter"
MAILRC="/usr/david/.mailrc"
MBOX="/usr/david/mbox"
asksub
asksubject
header
keep
chron
save
```

DEAD and **MAILRC** are system environment variables, while all the other parameters are mail variables.

DEAD Specifies directory and filename where messages are stored if an
interrupt occurs while you are running **mail**. The standard
definition is *$HOME/dead.letter*

MAILRC Specifies the name of the start-up-file. The standard definition is
$HOME/.mailrc.

The following is an example of possible settings in a user's *.mailrc* file. The
meaning of each variable is listed in the table following the example.

```
MBOX "/usr/david/mbox"
set asksub
set header
set keep
set save
set dot
set autoprint
set chron
set SHELL=/usr/bin/csh
```

Mail variables:

MBOX	Defines the path name and filename where the already read mail can be stored. The standard definition is *$HOME/mbox*.
set asksub	Sets **mail** to ask for a subject before you begin a mail message.
set header	Shows the beginning of the letters. By default, the header is activated.
set keep	Will not remove mailbox even if there are no messages. Instead, will set to zero.
set save	If an interrupt occurs, stores letters in the file *dead letter*.
set dot	Ends message composition and sends mail when . is typed at the beginning of any line.
set autoprint	Sets mail messages to print automatically each time you remove or save messages with the **undelete** command .
set chron	Displays messages in chronological order. By default, last message is displayed first.
set SHELL=*x*	Defines the shell in which you will use the mail system.

A *.mailrc* file can be created or edited with any ASCII editor such as **vi** . For more information on using **vi** see the article on **vi** , or Appendix B.

Sending binary files with mail

If you have 8-bit text files or binary files and you want to send them over a network, you may face problems. Data transmitted via **uucp** is often transmitted with only the lower 7 of a byte's 8 bits, depending on the hardware on the network. Older versions of TCP/IP and SMTP (Simple Mail Transfer Protocol) are based on 7 bit transfers. Some mail-forwarding programs also strip control characters, thus corrupting files.

There are two ways to send binary files with **uucp** and **mail**

1. Instruct **mail** to take standard input from a binary file rather than from the terminal keyboard by issuing a command like the following:
   mail peter < *binary file*, or
2. Use the UNIX commands **uuencode** and **uudecode**.

This first method is not reliable. The last method is the only method to prevent distortion and to prevent control characters from being stripped by mail. **uuencode** converts files from binary format into a stream of transmittable, 7 bit ASCII characters. **uudecode** converts a uuencoded file back into its original form. For more information, see the articles on uuencode and uudecode.

Files:

$HOME/.mailxrc	Personal start-up file for mailx-user.
$HOME/.mailrc	Personal start-up-file for mail-user.
$HOME/mbox	Alternative place for storage of electronic mail.
dead.letter	Unmailable text.
/etc/passwd	Sender identification and recipient locator.
/etc/mail/mailusr	Routing and name translation information.
$MAIL	Variable containing path name of mail file.

(*$HOME* is the environment variable set to your home directory.)

See also:
ls; mail; more; write; talk; uuencode; uudecode.

man
getting help for UNIX commands

To help you use the various UNIX commands, most UNIX systems include a built-in help function. SCO UNIX, Solaris and UnixWare support the command **man**.

When you enter **man** and a UNIX command, the system displays a full description of the different options and arguments which may be used with the command.

Command:
man [*options*] [*argument*]

Function:
Display reference entry for *argument*, which may be a command, file or other part of the UNIX operating system.

Options:

-a   (all). Displays all reference pages of all types matching *argument*.

-c   (col). Invokes **col** with **man** to filter control and other characters. Invoked automatically by **man** for screen display. If you save the manual page to a file you need to use the **-c** option to save the output in a readable format.

-p *pager*   (pager). Sets the type of pager used. The default is **pg.**

-t *formatter*   (formatter). Passes to *formatter* command for formatting. *formatter* can be any command script necessary for formatting the manual page on your terminal. By default, most systems use nroff.

Valid sections for **man** include the following:

ADM	System administration
C	Commands
CP	Programming commands
DOS	DOS subroutines and libraries
F	File formats
FP	File formats for programmers (Development System)
HW	Hardware dependent
LOCAL	Local utilities for your system
M	Miscellaneous
S	Subroutines and libraries

On some UNIX systems, you also find the help function **help**. If you enter **help**, you will get a menu-driven help system. If you are using such a system, ask your system administrator how the help function works.

mesg
permitting messages from other users

mesg sets access permission for the **write** command to write messages to your screen.

Command:
mesg [*option*]

Function:
Sets access permission for messages to the users terminal.

Options:

-y   (yes). Allows messages.

-n   (no). Stops messages except those from *root.*

mesg without any options displays the current **mesg** setting

Examples:
mesg y
Permits all users to write messages to your terminal.

mesg n
Stops all messages except those coming from the system administrator (*root*).

Note that **who -T** displays information about which users have messages set to yes.

Files:
/dev/tty*

See also:
mail; who; write; talk.

mkdir
making directories

mkdir is the command for making directories on a UNIX system. A directory is the basic working area in a UNIX filesystem. For example, each time you login to your account on your console or terminal, you are placed in your *$HOME* directory. This means that you will be situated in the directory area designated by the system for your use, (e.g. */home/david* or */usr/david*). Because you have write permission in your own user area, you can make subdirectories in that area. No matter where you are in the UNIX filesystem, if you have write permission, you can use **mkdir** to make new subdirectories.

Command:
mkdir [*option*] [*directory*] ...

Function:
Make a new directory.

Options:
-m   (mode). Specifies the mode of the new directory if different from the default set by **umask** (see **umask** below).

-p   (parent). Creates *directory* by creating all the non-existent parent directories first.

Arguments:
directory   Path and directory name of the directory you wish to create.

Example:

Let us suppose that David wants to create four directories: *wp, wingz, c* and *bin*. With **mkdir** (make directory) he can make directories and build up his tree structure. For example,
mkdir *wp*
Makes the directory *wp*

The other directories are made in the same way as *wp*. For example:

mkdir *wingz*
mkdir *c*
mkdir *bin*

Directories may alternatively be made by specifying their absolute path name. For example,
mkdir */usr/david/wp*

It is only necessary to use the full syntax if you are not situated in the parent directory of the new subdirectories.

The new directory structure cotains the following directories:
/usr/david/wp
/usr/david/wingz
/usr/david/c
/usr/david/bin

NOTE:

To make a directory, you must have write access to the parent directory. That is, you must have write access to the directory immediately above the new one in the directory structure.

See also:;

cd, directories, pwd, rmdir, umask.

more
display file contents

The UNIX command **more** displays the contents of a file one screen at a time. **more** is often used in connection with various other display and tool programs.

Command:
more [*option*] [*+linenumber*] [*+/pattern*] *file* ...

Function:
Displays contents of a file one screen at a time.

Options:

-c	Clears before displaying. Redraws the screen instead of scrolling for faster display.
-n	Sets the display to *n* lines per screen
-r	(return). Normally, **more** ignores control characters that it does not interpret in some way. The **-r** option causes **more** to display carriage returns as ^M..

When using **more**, more is shown at the bottom of the displayed screenas long as there is more of the file to display. **more** then waits for a command from the user. To see the next screen, press the space bar. Below, is a list of the commands most often used with **more**.

h or ?	Displays help.
<space bar>	(space bar). Displays next screen.
<Enter>	(Enter key) Scrolls the display one line at a time.
*n***f**	Jumps *n* screen forward.
*n***s**	Jumps *n* lines forwards.
/pattern	Searches for ***pattern.***
!command	Executes UNIX command (starts a shell).
q	Quits more.

Examples:

more */etc/termcap*
Displays content of file /etc/termcap one screen at a time.

more -r **.c*
Displays all the files ending with *.c* in the current working directory. The **-r** option causes the carriage returns to be displayed as ^M.

ps -ef | more
This command "pipes" the output of the **ps -ef** through **more** so that you see the running processes one screen at a time.

more -12 */etc/passwd*
Displays the contents of the file */etc/passwd.* Sets the screen window to 12 lines per screen.

more +15 */etc/hosts*
Displays */etc/host,* starting from line number 15.

more -20 +25 *datafile*
Displays the file *datafile,* starting on line 25. Sets the window size for each screen to 20 lines.

more +/qume */etc/termcap*
Displays */etc/termcap* and searches for the text, qume.

pg functions in much the same manner as **more**, but has a few more options. All options for the **more** command, are also accepted by **pg**. Note that UnixWare does not support the **more** command.

Files:
/etc/termcap; /usr/lib/more.help

See also:
cat; man; ps.

mv
move (or change names of) files

With **mv**, you can move a file from one directory to another, change its name, or both. You can also change directory names (to move directories to other locations in the filesystem, use **mvdir**) .If the file is given a name equal to the name of the destination file, the (old) destination file will be deleted before the file is moved.

Command:
mv [-f] *file1 file2*
or
mv [-f] *directory1 directory2*
or
mv [-f] *file1... directory*

Function:
Changes names of files or directories, or moves files. Directories may only have their names changed. To move directories, use the **mvdir** command (SCO UNIX and UnixWare).

Options:
-f   (force mode). Forces the move and suppresses error messages.

Arguments:
file1   Name of the file to be moved/changed (the original/source file).

file2   The new name of the file.

directory   New location for *file1.*

directory1   Name of the directory whose name is to be changed.

directory2   New name of the directory.

Examples:

mv *C1212345.key key*
This command changes the file with the name *C1212345.key* to *key*.

mv *unix* unixbook*
Moves all the files prefixed by *unix* to the subdirectory *unixbook/*.

mv */usr/tmp/letter /usr/david*
Moves the file *letter* in the directory */usr/tmp* to the directory */usr/david*. The filename remains the same.

mv */usr/david/wp /usr/david/word*
Changes the name of the directory */usr/david/wp* to */usr david/word*.

If *file1* and *file2* are placed in another file system, **mv** first copies and then removes the original file. The new file is owned by the user who moved it. If you try to **mv** a file that is not your own and that file is linked, **mv** will fail.

See also:
copy, cp, chmod; mvdir; rm.

mvdir
moving directory structures

As a system administrator, you can change the name and move a directory tree (a directory with its subdirectories and files) with the **mvdir** command (SCO UNIX and UnixWare only).

Command:
mvdir *source-directory destination-directory*

Function:
Moves a directory or directory tree.

Arguments:
source directory: The directory or directory tree to be moved.

destination directory: The new parent directory.

Example:

mvdir */usr/UII* */tmp*
This command moves */usr/UII* and all its subdirectories to */tmp* creating */tmp/usr/UII*

See also:
cp; copy; chmod; copy; mv.

newgrp
changing user group identity

A user may be a member of several groups. **newgrp** allows users to switch groups to any group they belong to in order to access files and commands only available to that group. All files created or stored after using **newgrp** take the name of the new group.

Command:
newgrp [*groupname*]

Function:
Changes the users active group.

Arguments:
Any group (defined in */etc/group*) that includes the user.

When you change groups with **newgrp**, a new shell is started up. For users using C-shell, the history table is zeroed. **newgrp** without any arguments changes the user back to their default group (defined in */etc/passwd*). To be able to change to another group, you must first be a member of one or more groups, as defined in */etc/group*.

After you change groups to your new group, you can access all the files and directories accessible to the new group members.

Example:

newgrp Support
Changes the user's group to **Support**. After this command, the user has access to **Support** group files and all files s/he creates have the group name **Support**.

See also:
chgrp; chmod; files.

news
reading system news

When you login to the system, your system may display a news message similar to the following:

news: Uniplex News.

This message indicates that there are two news items (**Uniplex** and **News**) available to all users. To see news items, enter the command
news
This command reads the news items stored in the directory *usr/news*.

Command:
news [-a] [-n] [-s]

Function:
Displays system news—usually defined by the system administrator.

Options:

-a   Displays the content of all the files.

-n   Displays the names of all the files.

-s   Displays the number of files placed in the directory *usr/news*.

The command without any options, shows all news items. The newest files are displayed first.

UNIX commands by example

Example:

news -a
Displays all the news items stored in the directory */usr/news*. A typical display
resembles the following:

```
Uniplex (root) Thu Dec 1  13:24:54 1994
The Application Uniplex 10.2 is installed
Regards from the system administrator

News (root) Thu Dec 22 14:24:10 1994
Remember to logout, the system will be taken down today at
06.00 pm!
Regards from the system adminstrator
```

Files:
   /etc/profile; */usr/news/**; *$HOME/.news_time*.

See also:
   Bourne shell; C-shell; Korn shell.

nice
changing process priorities

nice allows you to increase the priority of a given process. Increasing the priority of a process causes UNIX to allocate a larger part of the CPU resources. Thus, the process is executed faster. Conversely, reduced priority causes UNIX to allocate a smaller part of the CPU resources, and the process slows down.

The higher the priority number, the lower the priority. Priorities are specified with numbers ranging from 0 (highest) to 39 (lowest). The default priority is 20.

Most users can only decrease the priority of a program, they cannot increase it. To change a priority, a value is added to, or subtracted from the starting the priority number.

root can run programs with higher priority by using two negative signs. For example, the command

nice -- /sbin/SMTP

subtracts 10 (**nice** assumes the default number of 10 if you do not specify a value) from the original value of 20. The new priority number becomes 20-10=10. The program **/sbin/SMTP** then runs with a higher priority than the normal (20).

Command:
nice -/+*number* [*command*] [*command-argument* (if any)]

Function:
Changes the priority of a process by adding or subtracting a value to the priority number. Default priority number is 20 on a scale of 0 (highest) to 39 (lowest)—range may vary on non-Intel UNIX systems.

Options:
+/- *number*   *number* specifies the amount you want to increase or decrease your priority. The range is 1-19. If no number is specified, **nice** assumes a value of 10.

Arguments:
nice accepts any ***command*** and ***command-argument*** as arguments.

Examples:

nice -15 machine
The system adds 15 to the original value of the priority number. The new priority number for the program **machine** is 20+15=35.

nice /bin/calc
Because no number is specified, **nice** adds a value of 10. The new priority value becomes 20+10=30.

nice --10 /sbin/SMTP
Only the system administrator can start this program with this **nice** value. **nice** subtracts 10 from the original value of 20. The new priority number is 20-10=10. **/sbin/SMTP** is then run with a higher priority than normal (20).

See also:
nohup.

nohup
continue processes after logout

Normally, your processes started from a terminal (those run in both background and foreground) are automatically stopped when you log out, or if your terminal hangs up. If you have jobs that must be active after you have logged out, they must be started with **nohup** (no hang up).

Command:
nohup *command* [*command-argument*] **&**

Function:
Runs a command that ignores hangups and quits. **nohup** is used if you want a process to proceed after you have logged out of the system.

Arguments:
nohup takes any *command* and *command-argument* as an argument.

If the command displays output to screen and that output is not redirected, it is sent to the file *nohup.out*. If the user does not have write permission to the working directory, the output is sent to *$HOME/nohup.out*.

Examples:

nohup account 1987 > *result* **&**
Runs **account**. The number **1987** is an argument to **account**. Any eventual messages generated by account are sent to the file *result*.

nohup pstat | grep files > */tmp/number.o.filer* **&**
grep searches for the text string "files" in the output of the command **pstat**. The result is placed in the file */tmp/number.o.filer*. You can logout directly, without waiting for the result of the command to appear.

UNIX commands by example

nohup sortjob *datafile1 > datafile2* **&**
It is frequently desirable to use **nohup** to protect command scripts that recalculate databases. The command **sortjob** is used to sort and process *datafile1 > datafile2*.

See also:
chmod; nice; kill; processes; sh.

passwd
changing your password

If your system allows you to set your own passwords, you can use **passwd** to change your user password. To increase security, you should change your password frequently to stop intruders from entering or using your system.

Command:
passwd *username* [**-F** *filesystem*]

Function:
Changes passwords.

Options:

username   Changes password for ***username***. Only the system adminis- trator can change passwords for other users.

-F *filesystem*   Assigns passwords to filesystems. If supported, the system administrator can connect passwords to file systems.

passwd, with no arguments changes your own password.

Examples:

If you enter **passwd** and you already have a password and your system allows you to run the password generator, you see a screen resembling the following:

```
last    successful password change for kentd:
Sat Sep 4 17:18:57 1993
last unsuccessful password change for kentd:
Mon Jan 3 17:18:57 1993
```

```
Setting password for user: kentd
          Choose password

You can choose whether you pick a password,
or have the system create one for you.

     1. Pick a password
     2. Pronounceable password will be generated for you

Enter choice (default is 1):
```

If you press <**Enter**> or select **1**, you receive a prompt resembling the following:

```
New password
```

Enter your new password. It will not appear on the screen. Press <**Enter**> when you are done. Depending on the security level set for your system, your password will be checked for obviousness. If it passes the check, you receive the following prompt:

```
Re-enter new password:
```

Reenter your new password and press <**Enter**>. Your password has been changed.

Remember your password!
It is important to remember your password. Without the password you will not be able to login to the system. If you forget your password, you can ask the system administrator for a new password. Because all passwords are encrypted, the system administrator can not "look up" your old password.

A password normally consists of a minimum of 5 characters. It may consist of more than 14 characters, but only the first 14 characters (on some UNIX dialects it is 6 or 8) are significant. The password can never begin with a digit or a special character.

If the security level is set low enough SCO UNIX allows a password length of a minimum of 5 characters. UnixWare and Solaris sets the minimum at 6 characters. There are no upper limits, but only the first 8 characters are significant.

Depending on the security level you may be forced to wait a certain number of days before you are allowed to change your password. Similarly, you may also be forced to change the password after a certain time.

No password limitations are placed on *root* (the system administrator). *root* may change the password for all the other users. *root* can remove the password requirement for any user. If you are *root* and you want to change a given user's password, you must use the username as an argument to **passwd**. For example,
passwd laurad
Answer the prompts as in the first example. Press <**Enter**> only when the system requests the new password.

Default password parameters defined in the file */etc/default/passwd.*

paste
paste after cut

paste manipulates vertical parts of text files. This command is useful for treating data in tabular format. **paste** is used to vertically merge several files into one file. **paste** manipulates input files and sends the result to terminal. **paste** considers each individual file as a table with columns and connects them horizontally. The output is displayed on the screen unless it is redirected.

To use **paste** (and its counterpart **cut**), you have to know how the columns in a given file are separated. Usually the separator is a tab. However, **paste** allows you to use other characters as separators (e.g., a ":" or a space).

Command:
> **paste** *file1 file2* ...
> **paste -d** *list file1 file2* ...
> **paste -s** [**-d** *list*] *file1 file2* ...

Function:
Merge or "paste" selected vertical fields in a file. Use **paste** to paste files next to each other horizontally.

Options:
-d *list* The characters following **-d** are field separators You can specify a *list* of alternative separators. If you specify more than one separator **paste** cycles through them repeatedly. The default field delimiter is tab. If you use a space (or any other character with special meaning to the shell) as the field delimiter, it must be quoted.

The following may be used as field separators:

"\t"	tab
"\n"	newline
"\\"	backslash
"|"	vertical bar

-s   Merges subsequent lines instead of taking one from each input file. By default, **-s** uses a tab as separator. To use a different separator, use the **-d** option.

Examples (cut and paste):

Assume you have the following file, *datafile*:

```
Anne:040458:girl:9190.10.24566:Bank of Norway
Starni:040641:boy:8945.43.23457:Bank of Crete
Peter David:22-0759:boy:6072.55.34567:Bank of USA
Vigdis Aasta:090959:girl:2345.72.12675:Bank of Singapore
Nicholas Eric:010356:boy:9180.10.56543.Bank of England
```

datafile consist of 5 fields separated by the field delimiter " : ". The five fields are first name, birthday, sex, bank account number, and bank. If we issue the command
cut -f2,5 -d":" *datafile*
cut removes field numbers 2 and 5 in *datafile*. The separator or delimiter is ":" This command produces a screen display similar to the following:

```
040458:Bank of Norway
040641:Bank of Krete
220759:Bank of USA
090959:Bank of Singapore
010356:Bank of England
```

The command
cut -c1-3 *datafile*
lists the first three characters of the first column in the file *datafile*, or:

```
Ann
Sta
Pet
Vig
Nic
```

The following command
cut -d: -f1,5 */etc/passwd*
cuts out the username and the text fields from */etc/passwd*, producing a result resembling the following:

```
root:0000-Admin(0000)
daemon:0000-Admin(0000)
bin:0000-Admin(0000)
sys:0000-Admin(0000)
adm:0000-Admin(0000)
uucp:0000-uucp(0000)
nuucp:0000-uucp(0000)
nobody:uid no body
noaccess:uid no access
lp:0000-LP(0000)
listen:Network Admin
sysadm:general system administration
mhsmail:MHS Admin Processes
david:David Elboth
smtp:SMTP Processes
vigdis:vigdis Enge
```

Here is another example using both **cut** and **paste**:

First, use **cut** to separate the first names from the telephone list in the file *telephone*. *telephone* has the following contents:

```
david   2024537449
peter   3028345896
anne    4057493845
vigdis  6073743758
mark    2025496474
enid    1026532433
charles         4343434221
monica 5678432111
```

Use **cut** with the **-f** option to cut out the first field (first names) in the file *telephone* and put it into the file *firstname*.

cut -f1 *telephone >firstname*
To see the content of *firstname* use **cat.**

cat *firstname*
```
david
peter
anne
vigdis
mark
enid
charles
monica
```

Now use **paste** to combine the vertical tables. Let us make a new file named *newlist*, in which the telephone numbers are the first field and the first names the second. **paste** automatically separates the two columns with help of a tab character.

cut -f1 *telephone >name*
cut -f2 *telephone >number*
paste *number name >newlist*
cat *newlist*
```
2024537449    david
3028345896    peter
4057493845    anne
6073743758    vigdis
2025496474    mark
1026532433    enid
4343434221    charles
5678432111    monica
```

Now, remove the two data files:

rm *number name*

Your **cut** and **paste** job is complete.

Other **paste** examples:

paste -d":"*data1 data2* > *data*
Combines columns from the file *data1* with columns from the file *data2*. The new file is called *data*. The **-d** option defines the field separator as a colon (:).
ls | paste - - - -
Output from **ls** is piped to **paste. paste** displays the output on the screen (standard output) in four columns.

paste -s -d"\t\n" *namefile*
Combines two lines in the file *namefile* into one single line and displayed on the screen.

See also:

cat; cut.

ping
checking TCP/IP network connections

If you use TCP/IP, you can check network connections to other computers with **ping**. **ping** sends an echo request packet to any network hosts you use as an argument. If contact with the specified host is made, the data packet is returned.

Command:
ping [-sv] *computername*

Function:
Checks the network connection with a specified computer.

Options:
-s *packetsize* Specifies the size of the data packets. By default **ping** sends data packets of 56 bytes, that, when combined with the TCP/IP header information, translates into 64 ICMP data bytes. Varying the packet size is used to examine how packet transfer is working.

-v (verbose). If **-v** is set all packets received from *computername* are listed.

Arguments:
computername The name of the host to test network connections with.

Examples:

ping rothko
Attempts to make a network connection with the host named rothko.

---

ping 129.1.3.4
Attempts to make a network connection with the host identified by the Internet address, 129.1.3.4.

See also:
ftp; rcp; rlogin; rsh (rcmd); telnet.

Pipes and filters
Combining several commands

With the help of (what are called) "pipes", you can group together several commands. The result from one command is sent into another command for further processing. By using pipes, you may combine several small commands into one powerful command. In this way, you may begin to construct combinations of commands and create your own programs.

Basically, a pipe redirects the standard output of one command into a file and then uses the same file as standard input for another command. The symbol used for creating a pipe is "|" for pipe. The syntax for a pipe is the same for all UNIX shells.

Syntax:
   program.1 [*arguments*] | *program.2* [*arguments*]

Examples:

ls | lp -dapl6
The standard output from the **ls** command is sent (or "piped") to the **lp** command, which formats the output and sends it to the printer, **apl5**. To achieve the same result, a user would have had to issue commands resembling the following:

ls > *list*; **lp -dapl5** *list*; **rm** *list*
Here the output from **ls** is redirected to the file, *list*. A second command is executed (**lp -dapl5**) on the file, *list*. A third command is also necessary to remove the file, *list* (**rm** *list*).

ls -la | wc -l
Here the standard output from the **ls** command is piped to **wc**. The standard output from the **wc -l** command is the number of lines in the **ls** command.

cal | lpr
The standard output of the **cal** command is piped to the default printer.

UNIX commands by example

lf | wc -w
Here the standard output from the **lf** command is piped to **wc**. **wc -l** counts the number of words piped to it and displays the number of words produced by running **lf** on the current working directory

ls -la | more
The standard output of the **ls -la** command is piped through the filter, **more**. This command is particularly useful if there are more files than will fit on one screen in the current working directory.

sort *listing* **| uniq | lp**
The **sort** command sorts the file *listing*. The output of the sort is piped to the command **uniq** which sends all unique lines to **lp** which in turn formats them and sends them to the default printer.

ls -l */dev* **| sort -n +3**
This command displays a sort of the output of a listing of the */dev* directory.

cat */etc/passwd* **| wc -l >** *number.users*
This command counts the number of lines in */etc/passwd*, and places the result into the file, *number.users*. We could achieve the same effect by entering:

wc -l <*/etc/passwd* **>***number.users*
Here the command **wc -l** reads from */etc/passwd*. The result is redirected to the file, *number.users*.

Some programs are designed to be components of a pipe. Such programs are known as filters.

See also:
cpio; cut; find; grep; more; paste; pr; Redirection; sort; Standard input, standard output and standard error; tr; uniq.

pr
print filter for formatting pages

Use **pr** to display or print files. By default, **pr** displays files on the screen, but it can be used to send files to a printer if used in conjunction with the **lp** command. **pr** can also be used for formatting text before you send it to the terminal or printer. By default, **pr** prints 66 line pages including a 5 line header (consisting of the date, time and page number) a 56-line body text and a 5-line footer. Line 3 contains all the header information. The rest of the header and footer lines are blank. **pr** can display output in any number of columns up to the capacity of your terminal.

Command:
pr [*option*] [*file* ...]

Function:
Prints files.

Options:

+*n*   Begin printing with page *n* (default is 1).

-*n*   Prints *n* columns of output (default is 1).

-d   Double-spaces the output.

-h *header*   use *header* as header instead of the filename. If you use **-t** , then **-h** is ignored.

-m   Merges the specified files into one file. Files are printed one per column, i.e., file1 is placed into column 1, file2 into column 2, etc.

-p   Pauses before printing each page to the screen

-t   Suppresses the first 5 lines (header) and the last 5 lines (trailer) in the file(s).

-w*n*   Sets the width of a line to *n* characters. Default setting is 72. **-w** applies only to multicolumn output. There is no limit for single column output.

The options only affect how the file is displayed or printed. The source file or files are not changed.

Arguments:
Any filename(s) can be used as an argument.

Examples:

pr -3 *dataform*
Displays *dataform* in three columns.

pr -w70 *letter-offer*
Displays the file *letter-offer* with a width of 70 characters. Default width is 72. This is only relevant for multicolumn output. There is no limit for single column output.

pr -h "Order form 1995" *form1* **-h "Order form 2000"** *form2 form3*
Prints *form1* with the heading "Order form 1995". The files *form2* and *form3* are printed with the heading "Order form 2000".

pr -h "Order form 1995" *form1 form2 form3* I **lp -dlaser-III**
Merges *form1*, *form2* and *form3* and places the heading "Order form 1995" at the top of each page. The document is sent to the printer laser-III. The original files are not changed.

pr -3dh "Order form" *form1 form2*
Displays *form1* and *form2* in a double-spaced, three-column format with the heading "Order form".

pr -m -t -p -h "Prentice Hall" *Calc88 Calc89*
Merges and prints *Calc88* and *Calc89* in two columns. *Calc88* is placed into column 1 and *Calc89* into column 2. Headers and footers are suppressed. The header, Prentice Hall, is added to each page. **pr** pauses before displaying each page.

ls */usr/dave* | **pr -8 -w132** | **lp -dlaser-II**
pr formats the output from the ls-command into 8 columns with an overall width of 132 characters. The formatted output is sent to the printer laser-II.

See also:
cat; more; pg.

Print spooling

"Spooling" means using part of a hard disk for a storage area for files to be printed or transmitted. The print spooling system administers UNIX printing. SPOOL means Simultaneous Peripheral Operations On Line and allows UNIX to manage multiple print jobs simultaneously.

A print daemon manages the print operation. It queues the print jobs, stores them temporarily and sends them to the printer when it is their turn. The spooling system allows you to continue to work after you send a job to a printer. The spooling system makes it possible to send several jobs to a printer at the same time.

See also:
cancel; lp; lpstat.

Processes
UNIX processes

A process is one execution of a program and usually has a separate process identification number (PID). A process may start or spawn new processes as part of its operation (e.g., command shells). The original process is called the parent process; the new process is called the child. Normally, when a program is finished, every process belonging to it stops. A single process may include several different executing programs during its lifetime. A parent process can be terminated before its child process. If a parent is terminated before the child, the child process then inherits the PID of 1 (*/etc/init*).

The PID-number may have values within the limits 0-30000. All UNIX systems have an upper limit to the number of processes that can be active on the system at a time, as well as for how many processes one single user may have. These limits are set in the UNIX kernel.

The owner of a processes can terminate it with the **kill** command. The system administrator can terminate all processes.

User commands are processes. The UNIX shell (a process itself) reads and executes keyed-in commands. The shell initiates the execution, sends the arguments further and waits until it is ready before it displays a new prompt (ready message). To illustrate how this all works, let's take a look what happens when you issue a command like **echo**. For example,

echo "Hello"
`Hello`
The shell (Bourne shell, C-shell or Korn shell) reads the line echo "Hello", and parses (picks out) the command **echo** from the argument. Then,

1. The process is divided into two exact copies.
2. The parent process waits for the child to terminate.
3. The child swaps the old program (sh, csh, ksh) with the new (the command echo "Hello").
4. The child executes the program.
5. The child terminates.
6. The parent process goes on and the prompt is returned.

After you type the command (**echo** Hello) and press <**Enter**>, the process divides itself into two exact copies. For a process to be able to make a copy of itself, the function called **fork** is started. After a fork, you have two processes—one child process and one parent process. The difference between the two processes is that they have different PID numbers. The two processes share open files, and each process knows that it has a parent/child relationship to the other.

In our example, the parent tells the child that it will wait for the child to finish. This function is called **wait**. The child then determines that it must execute a new program. It then uses the function called **execute** (exec). The child swaps the old process (the shell) with the new (**echo**) The UNIX kernel frees the memory given to the old program and reads the new program. The new program writes its arguments to the standard output (the terminal). **echo** then executes the system call **exit** and terminates. After the child's termination, the waiting shell is revived. The parent process (your shell) returns and you see your prompt again.

Foreground and background processes

UNIX is a multi user, multiprocessing operating system. You can run a process in the foreground or in the background. If a process is running in the foreground, the command shell relinquishes control of the screen and waits until the process finishes before returning the prompt. If a process is run in the background, the command shell does not relinquish the screen. It returns the prompt before the child process completes its execution. If the process is run in the foreground, all the messages are displayed to the screen. Therefore, only one process can run in the foreground. You can run several background processes at the same time, but you should remember that all the output from background processes should be redirected away from the screen (to a file or to */dev/null*).

If the program runs in the foreground, the shell waits for the child process to terminate. When you initiate a background process, the shell does not wait for the child processes to be terminated. Instead it displays the process ID belonging to the child process and returns your prompt.

To start a foreground process, enter the program's name. The screen and keyboard are then associated with the foreground program. To initiate a background process, add an ampersand (&) character after the command or program name. When you start a process in the background, it receives its own process ID (PID) number. This number is displayed on the screen after you have given the command.

Note:
A background process cannot be run interactively.

Examples:

who > *test* &
Starts the processes associated with the command **who**. The result of **who** is sent to the file *test*. Since you have included an ampersand (**&**), the process is run in the background.

calc &
Starts the program **calc** and runs it in the background.

cc *wordpack.c* &
Compiles the C source code in the file *wordpack.c* in the background.

who | wc -l > *user.list* &
Pipes the result of **who** is piped to **wc -l**. The result is redirected to the file *user.list*. All of this is run in the background.

See also:
kill; nice; nohup; ps; time.

ps
viewing UNIX processes

Usually, a process is associated with a command or a program. Each process receives a unique process id number (PID) when started. **ps** generates a process status report that can help users and system administrators to more effectively manage their work environment.

All processes have a status which can change during execution. As long as the process is active, it will continue to have the same PID and run from the same shell. **ps** can be used to determine the PID number of hung or redundant processes which can then be removed with **kill**.

With **ps**, you can determine the status of all your processes.

Command:
ps [*options*]

Function:
Displays information about the active processes in the system.

Options:

- a	Displays all processes, except those associated with session leaders and processes not associated with terminals.
- l	Displays a long list.
- e	Displays all information about all active processes.
- f	Displays full listing of all processes.
- t *terminal*	Displays processes bound to *terminal* (tty).
- u *user*	Displays only those processes owned by *user.*

With the options **-ef**, you get a full listing. **ps** without any options, shows only the processes started by the user entering the command.

ps

Examples:

Solaris:
The command,
ps -ef
results in output resembling the following:

```
  UID    PID  PPID  C    STIME TTY      TIME COMD
root       0     0 80 12:20:36 ?       0:01 sched
root       1     0198 12:20:39 ?       0:01 /etc/init -
root       2     0  0 12:20:39 ?       0:00 pageout
root       3     0 80 12:20:39 ?       0:01 fsflush
root     176   161 10 12:21:34 ?       0:00 lpNet
root     206     1 80 12:21:39 console 0:01 -sh
root     111     1 18 12:21:15 ?       0:00 /usr/sbin/rpcbind
root     126     1 79 12:21:22 ?       0:01 /usr/sbin/inetd-s
root     103     1 41 12:21:14 ?       0:00 /usr/sbin/in.routed -q
root     113     1  4 12:21:16 ?       0:00 /usr/sbin/keyserv
root     117     1 19 12:21:16 ?       0:00 /usr/sbin/kerbd
root     129     1 20 12:21:23 ?       0:00 /usr/lib/nfs/statd
root     131     1 58 12:21:23 ?       0:01 /usr/lib/nfs/lockd
root     141     1  3 12:21:25 ?       0:00 /usr/lib/nfs/automount
root     148     1 80 12:21:28 ?       0:00 /usr/sbin/cron
root     169     1 27 12:21:33 ?       0:00 /usr/lib/sendmail -bd -q1h
root     330   206 11 12:59:12 console 0:00 ps -ef
root     161     1 40 12:21:33 ?       0:00 /usr/lib/lpsched
root     191     1 28 12:21:38 ?       0:00 /usr/sbin/syslogd
root     208   205 25 12:21:44 ?       0:00 /usr/lib/saf/ttymon
```

SCO UNIX:
The same command on SCO UNIX:
ps -ef
results in output resembling the following:

```
  UID    PID   PPID   C     STIME TTY    TIME   COMMAND
root       0     0     0   Nov 16 ?      0:00   swapper
root       1     0     0   Nov 16 ?      0:02   /etc/init
201       78     1     0   Nov 17 01     0:05   -csh
root      79     1     0   Nov 17 02     0:02   -sh
root      31     1     0   Nov 17 ?      0:00   logger /dev/error
root      30     1     0   Nov 17 ?      0:01   update
ps1       80     1     0   Nov 17 03     0:02   -csh
root      33     1     0   Nov 17 ?      0:01   cron
root      54    53     0   Nov 17 ?      0:02   ./rwhod
```

UNIX commands by example

For both UNIX versions, the meaning of the column headings is as follows:

UID	The owner of the process
PID	Process ID associated with the process. If you know the process ID, you can stop the process with the command kill
PPID	Parent process ID (if any)
C	% utilization of the system
STIME	Start time for the process
TIME	The total CPU time used up till now
TTY	The controlling terminal (device)
COMMAND	Name of the command/program

UnixWare

If you are running a UnixWare system, the command
ps -el
results in output resembling the following:

```
F S   UID   PID  PPID  C PRI NI    ADDR      SZ    WCHAN TTY    TIME COMD
39 S    0    0     0   0   0 SY  c07f7000     0  d0185616 ?    0:00 sched
10 S    0    1     0   0  39 20  c07f7048    37  e0000000 ?    0:01 init
39 S    0    2     0   0   0 SY  c07f7090     0  d104b200 ?    0:01 page
```

Processes are built hierarchically. Process number 0 is **sched** and belongs to *root*. This is the first process started by the operating system. The next process is **/sbin/init** —no. 1 (if you are running SCO UNIX, the name is **/etc/init**). This process is the mother of several processes e.g., pageout, lpNet, fsflush. Some processes also start other processes. In the first example (Solaris), process 176 is a child of the process 161.

The following command,
ps -t *tty1a*
produces output resembling the following:

```
PID TTY  TIME COMMAND
166  1a  0:02 csh
```

The terminal *tty1a*, has the process csh.

Files:

/UNIX	system list of names
/swap	swap
/dev/kmem	memory
/dev/mem	memory
/dev/ttxx	terminal name
/etc/passwd	UID information supplier

See also:

kill; nice; nohup; processes.

UNIX commands by example

pwd
print working directory

pwd (**p**rint **w**orking **d**irectory) prints the current working directory to screen. **pwd** displays the full pathname.

Command:
pwd

Function:
Displays the complete path name of the current working directory.

Options:
None. The Korn shell includes a different version of the same command.

Examples:

pwd
`/usr/david`
The output of the **pwd** command indicates that the user is currently working in the directory */usr/david*.

pwd
`/usr/spool/lp/interface`
pwd indicates that the user is currently working in the directory */usr/spool/lp/interface*.

See also:
cd.

rcmd (rsh)
executing remote commands

rcmd (SCO UNIX) and **rsh** (Solaris and UnixWare) allow users to execute commands on remote computer systems connected via TCP/IP. However, before any user can run a command on a remote system, the remote system must be set up to view the would-be user as equivalent to a local user on the remote system.

To create what is called "user equivalence" on a remote system, the user or system administrator must create an entry in the remote systems */etc/host.equiv* file (for establishing equivalence for the system as a whole) or in */$HOME/.rhosts* (for more limited equivalence).

These two files grant permission for remote users to use local user names without supplying local user passwords. If a home directory contains a *.rhosts* file, remote users on the remote systems specified in that file are equivalent to the local user. Each user specification in *.rhosts* contains the name of the remote host and the user for whom user equivalence is desired. For security reasons, a *.rhosts* file must be owned by the user granting user equivalence or by *root*. It can be writable only by the user granting the equivalence. If other users or groups have write permission to *.rhosts*, the contents are ignored by the system.

/etc/hosts.equiv is a list of remote hosts with matching name equivalence. The file lists remote hosts, one per line. For each host listed in */etc/hosts.equiv*, a remote user with the same name as a local user is equivalent to the local user. In effect, the users are the same if the names are the same. If you list a system in */etc/hosts.equiv*, make sure its security is as good as local security. One insecure system mentioned in */etc/hosts.equiv* can compromise the security of an entire network.

Command:
rcmd *computername* [-l *username*] [*command*]

Function:
Executes commands on remote TCP/IP hosts.

Options:

-l *username*   (login). Allows you to run the remote command as ***username***. By default, **rcmd** and **rsh** use the ***username*** of the user originating the command.

Arguments:

computername   Name of the remote system on which you want to run a command.

command   Name of the command you want to run on the remote system. If you do not specify a command, **rcmd** and **rsh** run **rlogin**.

Examples:

rcmd unixadmin ps -ef
Displays all the processes running on the system named unixadmin.

rcmd unixadmin lp -dverso < */etc/hosts*
Prints the local system's */etc/hosts* file on a printer controlled by unixadmin's (the remote system) spooling system

See also:

ftp; ping; rcp; rlogin; rsh; telnet.

rcp
copying a file over a network

The simplest way to copy files between two UNIX computers connected via TCP/IP is **rcp**. This command works in the same way as **cp** but requires that you specify the destination system name as well as the directory. Like **rcmd** and **rsh,** to execute a **rcp** command, user equivalence must be established in either */etc/hosts.equiv* or *HOME/.rhosts.* (For a discussion of *.rhosts* and */etc/hosts.equiv*, see **rcmd** or **rsh**.)

Command:
rcp [-rp] *filename(s) remotetarget*

Function:
Copies files to and from remote hosts running TCP/IP.

Options:

-r (recursive). If this option is specified and supported on your system, **rcp** will copy directory hierarchies recursively. If this option is used, *remotetarget* must be a directory.

-p preserve. Preserves the original modification times and modes.

Arguments:

filename(s) Name of file(s) to be copied. Note that **rcp** does not accept filename wildcards.

remotetarget The target can take any of the following forms:
user@remotehostname:path
remotehostname:path
or *path*

UNIX commands by example

Examples:

rcp unixadmin:*/usr/david/letter* .
Copies the file */usr/david/letter* from the system unixadmin to the current working directory on the local system.

rcp *offer* **unixadmin:***/usr/david/offer*
Copies the file *offer* from the local system to */usr/david* on the remote system unixadmin.

See also:
ftp; ping; rsh (rcmd); rlogin; telnet.

Redirection
Input, output and error

For each command a user issues, the shell (Bourne shell, C-shell or Korn shell) opens three files—standard input; standard output and standard error. By default, the standard input is the keyboard, and the standard output and standard error are the screen. The shell gives each standard file a number called a file descriptor. The shell uses 0 for standard input; 1 for standard output, and 2 for standard error. Higher numbers are reserved for any other files the shell has to open to complete a given command. Redirection means directing output to or input from a different file.

Redirecting output — >

The symbol ">" redirects UNIX output from the standard output (usually the screen) into a specified file. The file may be a device driver, which then sends the result to a printer, terminal, tape or floppy drive.

Syntax:
command or *program* [*argument*] > *file*

Example:

cat >*textfile*
Normally, **cat** with no arguments displays keyboard input on the screen. This command redirects the output of **cat** to *textfile*. If you list the contents of the current working directory, the file *textfile* now appears.

cat *del1 del2 del3* >*report*
Normally, **cat** displays the contents of the files *del1*, *del2* and *del3* on the screen. This command redirects the output of the **cat** command into a new file, named *report*.

> **ls** > *data*
> This command redirects the output of the **ls** command from the screen to the file *data*.

See also:

cat; Standard input, standard output and standard error.

Redirecting input — <

The symbol "<" causes UNIX to seek input from somewhere other than the standard input . Often that source is an input file. The specified file can be a device driver for a printer, terminal, tape or floppy drive.

Syntax:

command or *program* [*argument*] < *file*

> **Example:**
>
> **mail kentd** < *mailfile*
> This **mail** command sends input from the file *mailfile* rather than the keyboard to the user kentd. In this way, you can compose mail, using any editor you want, then send it.

See also:

Standard input, standard output and standard error.

Adding to a file — >>

The symbol ">>" causes redirected output to be added to the end of a file. The existing data in the file is untouched.

Syntax:

command or *program* [*argument*] >> *file*

> **Example:**
>
> **who >>** *data*
> Adds the result of the **who** command to the end of the file *data*.

See also:

Standard input, standard output and standard error.

Redirection and error messages

When standard input is redirected to a file, any error messages are still sent to the standard error (the screen). To redirect standard error messages, you must specify the file descriptor in the command. Thus, to redirect standard error messages to a specified file, use the syntax

2>filename

This argument directs the standard error to *filename.*

> **Example:**
>
> This example assumes two files—*myfile* and *superusersfile. myfile* belongs to *user* and *superusersfile* belongs to *systemadministrator. user* does not have read or write permission to *superusersfile*. The content of *usersfile* is the following:
>
> `Here is the textfile usersfile.`
>
> The owner of *usersfile* issues the following command:
>
> **cat** *usersfile superusersfile* **1>** *fileout* **2>** *fileerror*
> This command concatenates the contents of *usersfile* into the file *fileout*. The standard output of the **cat** command uses the file descriptor "1". **cat** also tries to read the contents of *superusersfile* into *fileout*. Because *user* does not have read permission to *superusersfile*, **cat** generates an error message which is redirected into the file *fileerror*. which uses the file descriptor 2. That is, **cat** generates the following error message:

```
cat: cannot open superuser
```
which is redirected into the file *fileerror*.

To redirect the standard error message into *fileout*, you could issue the following command:

cat *usersfile superusersfile* **1>** *fileout* **2>** &1
Directs the standard error message (**2>**) into *fileout* which is created from the standard output (**1>**).

Here is another example of redirecting output and error into the same file:

cat *usersfile superusersfile* **1>** *alldata* **2 >** &1

If you are using C-shell, you could also use

cat *usersfile superusersfile* **>** *alldata* **2 >>** *alldata*

In either case, *alldata* has the following contents:

```
Here we have the textfile usersfile
cat: cannot open superuser
```

See also:

Bourne shell; C-shell; Korn shell; Pipes and filters; Standard input, standard output and standard error.

restore
restoring file systems
(SCO UNIX and UnixWare only)

Archives made with **backup** are restored with **restore**. **restore** reads **cpio** format archives created by the **backup** command.

Command:
restore [-c] [-i][-o] [-t] [-d *device*] [*pattern* [*patterns*] ...]

Function:
Restores data archived with the backup program.

Options:

-c	(complete). Restores all files from backup media to disk.
-i	Displays the index file from the backup tape or diskette. This index file exists only if the backup was made with **backup.** The index file is a list of all the files on the backup media. **restore -i** displays a list of files, no files are restored.
-o	Overwrite existing files. If the file being restored exists, it is not restored unless this option is set.
-t	(tape). Restores from the tape device.
-d *device*	Specifies the *device* location of the backup

Arguments
pattern patterns When restoring files, one or more *pattern* or *patterns* can be used. The *pattern* is checked against the backup media and the file is restored if a match is found. Wildcards can be used to match multiple files. Since **backup** uses the full path name, **restore** places all restored files in their original location. If

you specify more than one *pattern*, place each pattern in quotation marks. If no *pattern* is specified, all files are restored. If the archive consists of more than one tape or floppy, the system prompts you as needed.

Examples:

restore -c -t
Restores all files from a tape archive.

restore -o -d */dev/rdsk/f03ht*
Restores all files from a floppy archive. If a file being restored already exists, it is overwritten with the file from the archive.

restore -i -d */dev/rmt/ctape1*
Displays the index from the tape in */dev/rmt/ctape1*. No files are restored.

restore -t */dev/rmt0*
This command restores all files from */dev/rmt0*

See also:

backup; copy; cp; cpio; dd; tar.

rlogin
using other computers on a network

rlogin (like **telnet**) connects your local terminal to a remote host. If you have established user equivalence on the remote machine, you may login remotely without specifying name or password. If not, the remote host prompts for user name and password.

To create what is called "user equivalence" on a remote system, the user or system administrator must create an entry in the remote systems */etc/host.equiv* file (for establishing equivalence for the system as a whole) or in */$HOME/.rhosts* (for more limited equivalence).

These two files grant permission for remote users to use local user names without supplying local user passwords. If a home directory contains a *.rhosts* file, remote users on the remote systems specified in that file are equivalent to the local user. Each user specification in *.rhosts* contains the name of the remote host and the user for whom user equivalence is desired. For security reasons, a *.rhosts* file must be owned by the user granting user equivalence or by *root*. It can be writable only by the user granting the equivalence. If other users or groups have write permission to *.rhosts*, the contents are ignored by the system.

/etc/hosts.equiv is a list of remote hosts with matching name equivalence. The file lists remote hosts, one per line. For each host listed in */etc/hosts.equiv*, a remote user with the same name as a local user is equivalent to the local user. In effect, the users are the same if the names are the same. If you list a system in */etc/hosts.equiv*, make sure its security is as good as local security. One insecure system mentioned in */etc/hosts.equiv* can compromise the security of an entire network.

Command:
rlogin [-l *username*] [*remotehost*]

Function:
Connects local terminal to remote host computer.

Options:
-l *username*   Use to login under a different username on the remote host.

Examples:

rlogin blueox
Requests a remote login on the system named blueox.

rlogin stjust -l *root*
Requests a remote login as *root* on the system named stjust.

See also:
ftp; ping; rcp; rsh (rcmd); telnet.

rm
remove files

rm removes files, directories or groups of files and directories. Removing files requires that you have write access to the directory. If you are the owner of the file, no other access privileges are required. **rm** supports the use of wildcards.

Command:
rm [-fri] [*file-or-directoryname*]

Function:
Removes files and directories.

Options:

-f   Removes write protected files without any warning.

-r   Removes all files recursively along with the directories themselves. **Use with extreme caution, esp. if you are root**.

-i   (interactive option). Prompts for confirmation before deleting files and directories.

Arguments:
file-or-directoryname   The argument can be any file(s) or directory(ies).

Examples:

rm *unix.fil*
Removes the file, *unix.fil*.

rm */bin/test*
Removes the file *test* from the directory */bin*.

rm -f *rep**
Removes all the files prefixed by rep. If any are write protected, **rm** removes them without warning.

rm -i *testdir*
Prompts you for removal before removing the file *testdir*.

rm -r */usr/david*
Removes all the files and subdirectories in */usr/david*.

rm -r ***
Removes all the files and directories starting in the current working directory and moving down the directory tree.

CAUTION:

The **-r** option is dangerous. Once started it will remove up to 17 levels of subdirectories. If you are logged in as *root* and issue the command in the wrong directory, you can seriously harm your system.

See also:

dosrm; rmdir.

rmdir
removing directories

rmdir removes directories if the following conditions are met:

- The directory contains no files.
- The directory contains no subdirectories.
- The directory is not the current working directory.

Command:
rmdir [*directoryname*]

Function:
Removes directories.

Arguments:
directoryname Path and the name of the directory to be removed.

Examples:

rmdir *wp*
Removes the *wp* subdirectory.

or, if you are not situated in the parent directory for *wp*. Use,

rmdir */usr/david/wp*

See also:
Directories; dosrmdir; mkdir; rm.

rsh (rcmd)
executing remote commands

rsh (Solaris and UnixWare) and **rcmd** (SCO UNIX) allow users to execute commands on remote computer systems connected via TCP/IP. However, before any user can run a command on a remote system, the remote system must be set up to view the would-be user as equivalent to a local user on the remote system.

To create what is called "user equivalence" on a remote system, the user or system administrator must create an entry in the remote systems */etc/host.equiv* file (for establishing equivalence for the system as a whole) or in */$HOME/.rhosts* (for more limited equivalence).

These two files grant permission for remote users to use local user names without supplying local user passwords. If a home directory contains a *.rhosts* file, remote users on the remote systems specified in that file are equivalent to the local user. Each user specification in *.rhosts* contains the name of the remote host and the user for whom user equivalence is desired. For security reasons, a *.rhosts* file must be owned by the user granting user equivalence or by *root*. It can be writable only by the user granting the equivalence. If other users or groups have write permission to *.rhosts*, the contents are ignored by the system.

/etc/hosts.equiv is a list of remote hosts with matching name equivalence. The file lists remote hosts one per line. For each host listed in */etc/hosts.equiv*, a remote user with the same name as a local user is equivalent to the local user. In effect, the users are the same if the names are the same. If you list a system in */etc/hosts.equiv*, make sure its security is as good as local security. One insecure system mentioned in */etc/hosts.equiv* can compromise the security of an entire network.

Command:
rsh *computername* [-l *username*] [*command*]

Function:
Executes commands on remote TCP/IP hosts.

Options:

-l *username*   (login). Runs the remote command as ***username***. By default, **rcmd** and **rsh** use the ***username*** of the user originating the command.

Arguments:

computername   Name of the remote system on which you want to run a command.

command   Name of the command to run on the remote system. If you do not specify a command, **rcmd** and **rsh** run **rlogin**.

Examples:

rsh unixadmin ps -ef
Displays all the processes running on the system named unixadmin.

rsh unixadmin lp -dverso < */etc/hosts*
Prints the local system's */etc/hosts* file on a printer controlled by unixadmin's (the remote system) spooling-system

See also:

ftp; ping; rcmd; rcp; rlogin; telnet.

sort
sorting data

sort sorts lines from standard input (the keyboard) or from a file or a set of files. Each line to be sorted can consist of numbers, single words, or a series of words and numbers. Each line is divided into fields separated by spaces (default) or by a character (set with the **-t** option). If you name more than one file, **sort** merges the files before the sorting begins. The result can be displayed in alphabetical, numeric or reverse (of either) order.

Command:
sort [*option*] *filename*.

Function:
Sorts (or merges and sorts) the content of files.

Options:

-d	Sort in dictionary order. Only letters, numbers, spaces and tabulators are significant with this option. This is alphanumeric sorting.
-f	Ignores case. If this option is set, there is no difference between uppercase and lowercase, e.g., "DANTON" and "danton".
-n	(numeric). Sorts the specified fields numerically, allowing for minus signs and zeros.
-r	(reverse). Sorts in decreasing (reverse) sequence.
-t*n*	Translates the field separator into *n*. For example, if you set the option, **-t:**, the field separator is a colon.
-u	(unique). If this option is set, **sort** overlooks the second of any repeated line.
-o*file*	(output). Send the output to *file.* Set this option to redirect output to a result-file (same as > *file*).

sort used by default (with no options) sorts by the first column in the file in
alphabetical order.

Examples:

who | sort
This command results in output resembling the following:

```
laura       tty02        Jul 11 06:15
johnnie     tty01        Jul 11 06:16
mary        tty03        Jul 11 06:15
root        tty03        Jul 11 06:15
```

The result from the **who** command is piped to **sort**. **sort** sorts the output
alphabetically based on the user name.

In the following examples, we create a data file for use with **sort**. First, we use **cat**
to make *datafile*.

cat > *datafile*
```
Anne Stahl:040458:girl:9190.10.34566:Bank of Norway
Starni Mooni:040641:boy:8945.43.23457:Bank of Krete
Peter David:220759:boy:6072.55.34567:Bank of USA
Vigdis Aasta:090959:girl:2345.72.23675:Bank of Singapore
Nicholas Eric:010356:boy:9180.10.56543:Bank of England
Control d
```

This file consists of the fields name, birthday, sex, bank account number and bank.
.: (colon) is the field-separator.

The command:
sort -f -t: *datafile*
displays the following:

```
Anne Stahl:040458:girl:9190.10.34566:Bank of Norway
Nicholas Eric:010356:boy:9180.10.56543:Bank of England
Peter David:220759:boy:6072.55.34567:Bank of USA
Starni Mooni:040641:boy:8945.43.23457:Bank of Krete
Vigdis Aasta:090959:girl:2345.72.23675:Bank of Singapore
```

The content of *datalist* is sorted alphabetically, based on the first data field. The : (colon) is the field separator. The sorting is not case sensitive.

Position parameters
To sort on differing data fields, you must specify field or position parameters. The notation *+pos1* and *-pos2* sets the sort field as the characters from beginning of *field1* until the end of *field2*. If *field2* is omitted, the end of the line is assumed.

Thus, the command:
sort -t: +2 *datafile*
displays the following:

```
Peter David:220759:boy:6072.55.34567:Bank of USA
Starni Mooni:040641:boy:8945.43.23457:Bank of Krete
Nicholas Eric:010356:boy:9180.10.56543:Bank of England
Vigdis Aasta:090959:girl:2345.72.23675:Bank of Singapore
Anne Stahl:040458:girl:9190.10.34566:Bank of Norway
```

The file was sorted based on the third field (sex).

The command
sort +1 -o *sortdata datafile*
creates *sortdata* with the following content:

```
Vigdis Aasta:090959:girl:2345.72.23675:Bank of Singapore
Peter David:220759:boy:6072.55.34567:Bank of USA
Nicholas Eric:010356:boy:9180.10.56543:Bank of England
Starni Mooni:040641:boy:8945.43.23457:Bank of Krete
Anne Stahl:040458:girl:9190.10.34566:Bank of Norway
```

datafile was sorted based on the second field. The field consisting of second name becomes field number 2, since no field-separators are specified. The result is placed into the file *sortdata*.

The command
sort -n +1 -t: -o *sortdata1 datafile*
results in the file *sortdata1* with the following content:
```
Nicholas Eric:010356:boy:9180.10.56543:Bank of England
Anne Stahl:040458:girl:9190.10.34566:Bank of Norway
Starni Mooni:040641:boy:8945.43.23457:Bank of Krete
Vigdis Aasta:090959:girl:2345.72.23675:Bank of Singapore
Peter David:220759:boy:6072.55.34567:Bank of USA
```

The file is sorted based on the second field. The specified field separator is **:** (colon). Since we specified the **-n** option, the sort is based on the numerical content of column number 2. The result is placed into the file *sortdata*.

The command
sort -t: +2n -3 */etc/passwd*
sorts the file */etc/passwd*. The results resemble the following:

```
root:x:0:3:0000-Admin(0000):/:/sbin/sh
sysadm:x:0:0:general system
administration:/usr/sadm:/usr/sbin/sysadm
daemon:x:1:12:0000-Admin(0000):/:
bin:x:2:2:0000-Admin(0000):/usr/bin:
sys:x:3:3:0000-Admin(0000):/:
adm:x:4:4:0000-Admin(0000):/var/adm:
uucp:x:5:5:0000-uucp(0000):/usr/lib/uucp:
lp:x:7:9:0000-LP(0000):/var/spool/lp:/sbin/sh
listen:x:37:4:Network Admin:/usr/net/nls:/usr/bin/sh
smtp:x:100:6:SMTP Processes:/var/spool/smtpq:/usr/bin/sh
vigdis:x:101:1:vigdis Enge:/home/vigdis:/usr/bin/ksh
david:x:202:1:David Elboth:/home/david:/usr/bin/sh
nobody:x:60001:60001:uid no body:/:
noaccess:x:60002:60002:uid no access:/:
```

This command sorted the password file based on numerical user names. These are found in the third column. The field separator is set to be **:** (colon).

Standard input, standard output and standard error

Standard input, standard output and standard error are the building blocks of UNIX command structures. By default, standard input comes from your keyboard. Most UNIX commands write their data to your screen display which is the standard output. A program or a command may also send data to a hard disk, printer, floppy disk or tape. If an error occurs, an error message is sent to the standard error device (usually your screen) .

Standard input, standard output and standard error have three different numbers called file indicators:

0	standard input (**stdin**)
1	standard output (**stdout**)
2	standard error device (**sterr**)

These file indicators can be connected to data files. All may be redirected. For example, output may be redirected to a file, a printer or another terminal.

Data can be redirected to various physical units. This is done by redirecting the data to device files associated with the various units. These files are called device drivers and are situated in the directory */dev*. For example, */dev/tty5a* represents a terminal and */dev/lp* represents your computer's parallel port.

Both the standard input and standard error device can be redirected to various units. Redirection may also change the file indicators belonging to a process.

With the use of a pipe, data from one command can be directly fed into the input of another command.

Examples:

command > *file*
Sends standard output from a command to a file.

command >> *file*
Appends standard output to a file.

command 2> *file*
Sends standard error to *file*.

command 2>> *file*
Appends standard error to *file*.

command < *file*
Reads standard input from *file*.

command << *word*
Reads the text from standard input until it finds the first occurrence of the text "word".

command.1 | command.2
The result of **command.1** is piped to **command.2**

See also:

Redirection; Pipes and filters.

UNIX commands by example

stty
set terminal parameters

stty (set tty) informs the kernel of terminal and communications line parameters. This utility specifies the data communications speed of the terminal, enables parity checking to be performed, and designates characters to be used to backspace or send break signals. stty establishes or modifies the behavior of UNIX terminals.

Command:
stty [-a] [-g] [options]

Function:
Sets or alters the options for a terminal.

Options:

-a	Reports all option settings.
-g	Reports current settings in hexadecimal format.
0	Hangs up phone line immediately.
50,,19200	Sets terminal baud rate to the specified number.
cs5 cs6 cs7 cs8	Displays the selected character size (5-bit, 6-bit, 7-bit, 8-bit).
cstopb	Uses two stop bits per character.
-cstopb	Uses one stop bit per character.
echo	Displays all the entered characters on the screen.
istrip	Strips all ingoing characters to 7 bits.
-istrip	Does not strip ingoing characters.

ixon	Enables START/STOP output control. When enabled, output stops by sending a STOP control character and starts by sending a START control character.
-ixon	Disables START/STOP output control.
ixoff	Requests that the system send START/STOP characters when the input queue is nearly empty or full.
-ixoff	Requests that the system not send START/STOP characters when the input queue is nearly empty or full.
onlcr	Maps newline to carriage return and newline on output.
-onlcr	Does not map newline to carriage return and newline on output.
opost	Post-processes output.
-opost	Ignores all other output modes.
parenb	Enables parity generation and detection.
-parenb	Disables parity generation and detection.
sane	Resets all modes to reasonable values.
tabs	Preserves tabs when printing.
-tabs	Expands tabs to spaces.

Many more options are available. Refer to your man pages for a full listing. If no arguments are specified, the **stty** command displays the set-up of your terminal.

Examples:

stty
Displays the following output:

```
speed 9600 baud;    ispeed 9600 baud;    ospeed 9600 baud;
-parity hupcl
swtch = ^@; susp = ^@;
brkint -inpck -istrip icrnl onlcr
echo echoe echok
```

stty 9600
Sets your terminal's baud rate to 9600.

stty -a < */dev/ttyp02*
Displays the settings of ttyp02.

stty 9600 < */dev/ttp02*
Sets the baud rate to 9600 on ttyp02.

stty intr ^c
Sets the break send key to **<Ctrl>c** on your terminal.

stty erase ^h
Sets the erase key to **<Ctrl>h** on your terminal.

stty sane
Resets all the parameters to default values on your terminal.

stty tabs
Informs the system that your terminal expands tab characters; they will pass directly through the terminal handler to be expanded by your terminal.

stty 9600 cs7 parenb
Sets speed to 9600 baud, 7-bits character size and turns on the parity bit.

stty -ixon -istrip cs8
START/STOP output control does not strip input characters to 7 bits in order to use an 8-bit character set.. You can use this statement if you running a 8 bit application over TCP/IP or IPX/SPX (SCO).

stty -istrip cs8 opost onlcr
Does not input characters to 7 bits in order to use an 8-bit character set, and post-processes the output. You can use this statement if you running a 8 bit application over TCP/IP or IPX/SPX (Sunsoft).

talk
talk to another user

talk is a powerful variant of **write**; it allows you to send lines of text from your terminal to that of another user. The recipient does not have to be logged on to the same host, and you can both type to each other simultaneously.

Command:
talk *username* [*ttyname*]

Function:
Sends messages to and from logged-in users.

Options:
ttyname   Sends message to the specified terminal if the user is logged in more than once.

Arguments:
The user's login name.

Examples:

To start a talk session with someone on the same machine, specify the recipient's login name:

talk todd
In this example, todd is the login name of the person with whom you wish to communicate.

If the recipient is logged in to another host, you must specify *username@host*. If todd were logged into a host named "halogen," you would type the following:

talk todd@halogen
If the user is logged in more than once, specifying the *ttyname* will send your message to the appropriate terminal:

talk todd@halogen *tty8a*

talk sends this message to the recipient's terminal:

```
Message from TalkDaemon@user's_machine ...
talk:  connection requested by your_login@your_machine.
talk:  respond with: talk your_login@your_machine
```

If the recipient wishes to respond, he/she should reply accordingly. Both parties will then be connected and can type to each other simultaneously—the output will appear in two separate windows. Type **<Ctrl>l** to redraw the screen; send an interrupt character to exit the program.

The **mesg** command can be used to prevent talk requests from appearing on your terminal.

Files:
/etc/utmp	find the user's tty
/etc/hosts	find the user's machine

See also:
mail; mesg; who; write.

tar
archive and restore files

tar ("tape archive") saves and restores data to and from an archive medium, usually a floppy disk or tape. tar's actions (that is, in what manner/format the data will be copied, which device driver will be used, and so forth) are decided with the use of key parameters. If a device driver is not specified, tar uses the default device specified by the entry archive in */etc/default/tar*.

Command:
tar [Abxucvfpt] [*device*] [*files*]

Function:
Copies files to and from a backup medium.

Options:

A   Suppresses absolute file path names, causing all path names to be interpreted relative to the current working directory.

b   Uses the next argument as a blocking factor. The standard block factor is usually 20 (1 block = 1 Kbyte). This option is often used in connection with magnetic tapes.

x   Extracts the specified files from the archives. If a name corresponds to a directory, the directory is read and placed recursively on the disk. Copying is done according to the same hierarchical directory structure as the original. If a filename is not specified, the full tape (medium) is restored to disk.

u   Updates the specified files, if they are not included already or if the files have been modified since they were last archived.

c   Creates a new archive and is used the first time data is copied to a diskette or tape. All the previous data on the tape is removed.

v	Displays the names of each file or directory that it processes. Usually **tar** does not display this information.
f	Uses the next argument as the device name instead of the default (*/dev/rfd0*).
p	Extracts files with the original owner attributes and ignores the present value returned by **umask**.
t	Displays the specified filenames as they occur on the archive.

Arguments:

Depending on the options specified, the argument can be a *filename* or a *devicename*.

SCO UNIX examples:

tar cvf */dev/rfd0 textfile*
Copies the file *textfile* to a diskette. If *textfile* is a directory, the full directory is copied to diskette. **c** indicates that a new archive will be created on the diskette, **v** indicates that the copying itself will be displayed, **f** followed by the device driver gives the destination (*/dev/rfd0*) of *textfile*.

tar cvf */dev/rfd048ds9 /usr/peter*
Copies all files and directories under */usr/peter* to diskette.

tar cvf */dev/rmt0 /usr*
Copies all files and directories under */usr* to tape.

tar xvf */dev/rfd0*
Copies everything from diskette and restores to the hard disk. The directories and files are placed in their original locations on the hard disk.

tar xvf */dev/fd048ds9*
Specifies a different driver (360 Kbyte).

tar tvf */dev/rfd0*
Shows only the contents of the diskette.

UNIX commands by example

tar tvf */dev/rfd096ds15*
Displays only the contents of a 1.2 Mbyte diskette.

tar cvf */dev/rmt0 /usr/david /bin/prog*
Copies the files */usr/david* and */bin/prog* to tape. */dev/rmt0* is the system's
device driver. (Device drivers are commonly designated as */dev/rct0*, */dev/rct1*,
/dev/rmt0, */dev/rmt1*, */dev/rctmini,* etc.)

tar cvf */dev/rmt0 ./UII*
Copies the directory UII to tape.

tar cvf */dev/rmt1 .*
Copies the current working directory to /dev/rmt1.

tar xvf */dev/rmt0*
Performs a restore from tape to hard disk.

UnixWare examples:

tar cvf */dev/rdsk/f05ht* *
Copies all files and directories to diskette. The driver refers to a diskette possessing
a format of 1.2 Mbytes.

tar cvf */dev/rdsk/f15d9 UII*
Copies the textfile or directory UII to diskette with a format of 360 Kbytes. The
diskette is placed in the second disk drive.

tar cvf */dev/rdsk/f03ht* *
Copies all files and directories to diskette. The driver refers to a diskette having a
format of 1.44 Mbytes.

tar cvbf 15 */dev/rmt/rct0* *
Copies all files and directories to tape. The blocking factor is 15. The **b** option
instructs the tar command to use the next argument as a blocking factor. Thus, 15
blocks (15 Kbytes) are allocated.

tar cvf */dev/rdsk/f03ht /usr/philip /usr/david*
Copies the directories */usr/philip* and */usr/david* to diskette.

tar xvAf */dev/rdsk/f03ht*
Places files copied from diskette to hard disk in the current directory (the directory where you are working and executing **tar**).

tar tvf */dev/rdsk/fd03ht*
Displays the contents of a 1.44 Mbyte diskette.

tar cvf */dev/rmt/ctape1 /home/david /home/vigdis*
Copies the directories */home/david* and */home/vigdis* to tape.

tar cvf */dev/rmt/ctape1 ./UII*
Copies the directory *UII* to tape.

tar cvf */dev/rmt/ctape1 .*
Copies the current working directory to */dev/rmt/ctape1* (tape).

tar xvf */dev/rmt/ctape1*
Performs a restore from tape to hard disk.

Solaris examples:

tar cvf */dev/rdiskette* *
Copies all files and directories to diskette. The drive refers to a diskette having a format of 1.44 Mbytes.

tar cvf */dev/rdiskette /home/peter /home/ann*
Copies the directories */home/peter* and */home/ann* to diskette. The drive refers to a diskette having a format of 1.44 Mbytes.

tar cvf */dev/rmt/0 /home*
Copies the directory */home* to tape.

tar tvf */dev/rdiskette*
Displays the contents of a 1.44 Mbyte diskette.

UNIX commands by example

tar cvf */dev/rdiskette* */home/david/calc* */home/vigdis/text*
Copies the directories */home/david/calc* and */home/vigdis/text* to diskette.

tar cvf */dev/rmt/0* */usr/oracle7*
Copies the directory */usr/oracle7* to tape.

If no archive device is specified, **tar** looks in the */etc/default/tar* file for device drivers.

/etc/default/tar for SCO UNIX:

```
#        device             block  size   tape

archive0=/dev/rfd048ds9      18    360    n
archive1=/dev/rfd148ds9      18    360    n
archive2=/dev/rfd096ds15     10    1200   n
archive3=/dev/rfd196ds15     10    1200   n
archive4=/dev/rfd096ds9      18    720    n
archive5=/dev/rfd196ds9      18    720    n
archive6=/dev/rfd0135ds18    18    1440   n
archive7=/dev/rfd1135ds18    18    1440   n
archive8=/dev/rct0           20    0      y
archive9=/dev/rctmini        20    0      y
archive=/dev/rfd096ds15      10    1200   n
```

/etc/default/tar for Solaris:

```
#        device          block  size
archive0=/dev/rmt/0       20     0
archive1=/dev/rmt/0n      20     0
archive2=/dev/rmt/1       20     0
archive3=/dev/rmt/1n      20     0
archive4=/dev/rmt/0       126    0
archive5=/dev/rmt/0n      126    0
archive6=/dev/rmt/1       126    0
archive7=/dev/rmt/1n      126    0
```

/etc/default/tar **for USL (UnixWare)**:

```
#       device                 block  size
archive0=/dev/rdsk/f05dt    18     360
archive1=/dev/rdsk/f15dt    18     360
archive2=/dev/rdsk/f05ht    15     1200
archive3=/dev/rdsk/f15ht    15     1200
archive4=/dev/rdsk/f03dt    18     720
archive5=/dev/rdsk/f13dt    18     720
archive6=/dev/rdsk/f03ht    18     1440
archive7=/dev/rdsk/f13ht    18     1440
archive8=/dev/rmt/c0s0             20     0
#archive9=/dev/null #reserved
#
# The default device in the absence of a
#  numeric or "-f device" argument
archive=/dev/rdsk/f05ht     15     1200
```

tar xv6
Copies the total contents of a 1.44 Mbyte diskette (only SCO and UnixWare) placed in the first disk drive to disk. Since the **v** option is specified, every extracted file and directory is displayed to screen.

tar cv7 */usr/UII/Tcap*
Copies the textfile */usr/UII/Tcap* to a 1.44 Mbyte diskette placed in the second disk drive. The result is displayed.

tar tv2
Displays the contents of a 1.2 Mbyte diskette placed in the first disk drive.

You can find the default tar settings on your system in */etc/default/tar*.

See also:
backing up UNIX systems; backup; copy; cp; dd; restore.

telnet
communicate with other computers on a network

telnet is a terminal emulation program using the TELNET protocol that allows you to connect to other computers.

Command:
telnet [*computer_name*]

Function:
Acts as an interface for communicating with a remote system.

Options:
See your UNIX reference handbook.

If no computer name is specified, **telnet** invokes a command mode. (The `telnet>` prompt will appear.) You can execute numerous commands in this mode; a few are listed below:

`telnet>`**help**
Provides a complete listing of existing commands.

`telnet>`**close**
Terminates a telnet session.

`telnet>`**quit**
Terminates **telnet**.

Examples:

telnet blueox
```
Trying ...
Connected to blueox.sco.com.
Escape character is '^]'.

UNIX System V Release 3.2 (blueox.sco.com) (3.2)
```

In this example, **telnet** connects to the system "blueox" and brings up a login prompt.

See also:
ftp; ping; rcp; rlogin; rsh (rcmd).

time
time a command

time displays the amount of time elapsed during a command or program execution.

Command:
time *command*

Function:
Calculates how much time the UNIX system uses to execute a command or program.

Arguments:
UNIX command or program.

When the **time** command is executed, the following information is provided:

- Time elapsed for the command itself (real), displayed in seconds. The time is calculated from the moment you start the command to the time your prompt returns to your screen.

- Time used for the user program's execution in the system (user).

- Time spent on execution of the command/programs in the system (sys).

Examples:

```
time du >tmp.file
real    27.6
user     0.8
sys      9.1
```

The first number in this example shows that it took 27.6 seconds before the command was executed. The internal load of the system used 0.8 seconds. Thus, the remainder of the time was used to execute I/O (reading of the hard disk). 9.1 gives the program's utilization in seconds.

time cc pc8iso8.c
```
pc8iso8.c
3.8u 2.2s 0:09 66%
```

Calculates the time used for a compilation. (This example is taken from a C-shell session (csh). The displayed information may be somewhat different depending on the shell program you use.) The internal time the **cc** command uses for the compilation is 3.8 seconds. The program's utilization takes 2.2 seconds. The total use of time for the command is 9 seconds, and the program's utilization of the system is 66%.

tput
check the terminfo database

tput allows the user's shell to access the values found in the terminfo database. Depending on the option, **tput** can allow the shell (or shell script) to reset the terminal or to display the long name of the requested terminal type. **tput** outputs a string if the attribute is a string, or a number if the attribute is a number. If the attribute is Boolean, **tput** sets the exit code (0 for TRUE if the terminal has the capability, 1 for FALSE if it does not) and produces no output.

Command:
tput [-T*type*] [*termcode* (*function*)]

Function:
Displays the operation capabilities of your terminal using the contents of the terminfo database.

Options:
-T*type*   Specifies the terminal *type*. Specifies the default value of the environment variable, **TERM**.

The following options use the form:

termcode	*function*
clear	clears the screen sequence for the current terminal
cols	prints the number of columns for the current terminal
bell	gives bell sound from the terminal
blink	blinks
dim	dims the terminal screen
smul	starts underline
rmul	stops underline
sgr0	turns off all the codes

Examples:

tput dim
Dims the screen.

tput clear
Clears the screen.

tput sqr0
Turns off all the codes.

echo "`tput smul` "This is a text with underline `tput rmul`"
Displays text using underlines.

See also:
echo.

tr
translate characters

The **tr** command copies the standard input to standard output with substitution or deletion of selected characters. Input characters found in *string1* are mapped into the corresponding characters of *string2*. The text is read from default input or from file. The result is sent to default output if nothing else is specified.

Command:
tr [-cds] [*string1*] [*string2*]

Function:
Translates or deletes characters while copying from standard input to standard output.

Options:

-c   Inverts characters given by *string1*.

-d   Deletes all input characters given by *string1*.

-s   Squeezes a certain number of repeating characters in *string2* into single characters.

Input is specified by *string1* and the result by *string2*.

Examples:

tr -s "\012" < *datafile*
Removes all empty lines in the file *datafile*.

tr "[A-Z]" "[a-z]" < *datafile*
Converts all capital letters in file *datafile* into lowercase.

---

echo "This is UNIX World" | tr U X
```
This is XNIX World
```
In this example, the **tr** command replaces U by X in the text string "This is UNIX World."

See also:

sh.

tty
display terminal name

The **tty** command displays a terminal's path name on standard output.

Command:
tty [-s]

Function:
Prints the name of the specified terminal's device driver.

Options:
-s   Suppresses the printed output so you may test just the exit code.

Examples:

tty
```
/dev/tty01
```
The device driver used for this terminal session is */dev/tty01* (SCO).

tty
```
/dev/pts003
```
The device driver used for this terminal session is */dev/pts003* (UnixWare).

---

uniq
remove duplicate lines of text

If you wish to remove duplicate lines of text in a file, the **uniq** command will come in handy. **uniq** reads from input and compares only adjacent lines. If **uniq** comes across repeated lines, it removes all but the original occurrence.

In many instances, your file will contain duplicate lines that are scattered throughout. In this case, you can first use the **sort** command in order to arrange all duplicate lines adjacent to each other.

Command:
uniq [-udc[+n] [-n]] [input [output]]

Function:
Removes duplicate lines as long as they are adjacent to each other.

Options:

-u	Displays just the lines that are non-repeating.
-d	Displays one copy only of repeated lines.
-c	Precedes each line by the number of times it is repeated.
-n	Ignores the first *n* fields and blanks.
+n	Ignores the first *n* characters.

Examples:

sort *datafile* **| uniq**
First, sorts the datafile, then removes all duplicate lines.

sort *datafile* **| uniq -c**
Displays the number of repeated lines.

See also:
sort.

uudecode
decode a binary file

uudecode decodes a binary file after transmission. It strips from an encoded file any leading and trailing lines added by mailer programs and recreates the original binary data with the correct filename, mode, owner, and group. (The name of the original file is defined in the encoded file.)

Command:
uudecode [*encoded-file*]

Function:
Decodes an encoded file to a binary file or an 8-bit text file.

Example:

uudecode < *letter.7bit*
uudecode reads the uuencoded file and recreates the original binary file, giving it the name specified in the header line, which may differ from the name of the uuencoded file. The above example may produce a file called *letterto.susan* if that filename is specified in the header line of *letter.7bit*.

See also:
mail; uuencode.

uuencode
encode a binary file

uuencode converts any binary file into a stream of transmittable, 7-bit ASCII characters that can be transferred via uucp or other electronic mail delivery systems.

Command:
uuencode [*sourcefile*] [*remotefile*]

Function:
Encodes a binary file or an 8-bit text file to a 7-bit ASCII file.

Arguments:

sourcefile   Original file to be encoded. If this argument is not specified, **uuencode** reads from the standard input as the default.

remotefile   The name the file will be given at the remote site after it has been uudecoded. You must always supply this argument. It is advised that you give the file to be uuencoded a different name at the remote site to prevent the unfortunate accidental overwriting of existing files.

Examples:

uuencode *letter.8bit letterto.susan* > *letter.7bit*
Converts the 8-bit file *letter.8bit* to the 7-bit file *letter.7bit*. The filename (*letterto.susan*) is now defined in the heading of the file *letter.7bit*. When the file is uudecoded, the 8-bit file will be named letterto.susan.

You can also pipe the result of the command directly into mail:

uuencode *grad.form contract.ship* | **mail Berkeley!susan**
Converts the 8-bit binary file *grad.form* to 7-bit. The output is piped to the mail program, which sends the file to the user *susan* on a machine called *Berkeley*. When the mail is decoded with the **uudecode** program, the name of the 8-bit file is *contract.ship*.

See also:
mail; uudecode.

umask
set file creation code

Each time a file or a directory is created, a certain code is automatically set up to define the user's access rights. This code is the file's umask value.

Masks are made up of three-digit octal numbers that represent the owner, the group and all other users, respectively.

In the Bourne shell, **umask** is located in *.profile*. In C-shell, **umask** is located either in *.login* or in *.cshrc*. In the Korn shell, **umask** is set up in *.kshrc*.

Command:
umask [*argument*]

Function:
Sets the default access code for files.

Arguments:
Three digits; the maximum value for each of the digits is 7. The relationship between decimal, octal, and binary values is shown here:

Decimal Value	Octal Value	Binary Value
0	0	000
1	1	001
2	2	010
3	3	011
4	4	100
5	5	101
6	6	110
7	7	111

0 = the access code is switched on
1 = the access code is switched off

If arguments are not specified with the **umask** command, the current umask value will be displayed.

Examples:

umask 073
If you set the umask value to 073, all files created will allow rwx (readable, writable, executable) access permissions for the owner, no access for members of the group, and read access only for all other users.

umask 022
Shows the current umask value. The file owner has read and write permissions; the group and all other users have only read access.

umask 042
Sets the **umask** value to 042. Members of the group have write access, and all other users have read access. The file owner has both read and write access.

See also:
chmod, csh; files, sh.

uname
print system name

uname supplies useful information about an operating system, hardware, and communications network. Without options, it prints the current system name of the UNIX system on standard output.

Command:
uname [-snrvma]

Function:
Displays the UNIX system name, the name of the node for your UNIX computer and CPU type.

Options:

-s	Displays the name of the system.
-n	Displays the name of the node. This name is used as a reference when network communication is used.
-r	Displays the release number of the UNIX operating system, for instance, V.3.2 or V.4.2.
-v	Displays the version of the UNIX operating system. If you are running V.4.2, **-v** displays the number 2.
-m	Displays the hardware in use, for example, i386 or SPARC™.
-a	Prints all information.

Examples:

uname -s
`UNIX`
Shows the system name is UNIX.

uname -a
```
blueox blueox 3.2 2 i386
```

Displays the following: the system name (*blueox*), the node name (*blueox*), the release (3.2 2), and the computer architecture (i386).

uname -a
```
UNIX_SV david 4.2 1 i386 386/AT
```

Shows the system name (*UNIX System V*), the node name (*david*), the release (4.2 1), the computer architecture (i386), and the bus (386/AT).

vi
screen editor

vi is a powerful screen-oriented display editor that allows you to edit text files with a host of simple and (mostly) mnemonic commands. For more information, please refer to Appendix B.

UNIX commands by example

wall
write to all users

    wall sends a message preceded by the words "Broadcast Message..." to all logged-in users. You must be superuser to use this command; this is so you can override any protections the users may have invoked. This command is a good way of notifying your users of impending system shut-downs and the like.

Command:
    wall [*filename*]

Function:
    Reads a message from standard input until an end-of-file. **wall** overrides the **mesg** command.

Arguments:
    filename   Name of file to be broadcast.

Example:

wall
The swallows are returning to Capistrano—log out immediately.
<Ctrl>d

The system users will see the following:

```
Broadcast Message from root (tty01) on blueox   Feb 20 15:53 1994...
The swallows are returning to Capistrano-log out immediately.
```

Files:
    /dev/tty*.

See also:
    mail; mesg; who; write; talk.

who
list users logged in

The handy **who** command shows which users are using the system. In addition to displaying their logins, **who** lists the terminals they are logged in to, the time they logged in, the elapsed time since activity occurred, and process IDs for all active processes. **who** with the **am i** option identifies the user who invokes the command.

who gathers its information from the */etc/inittab* and */etc/utmp* files.

Command:
who [**-ulTqa**]
who am i

Function:
Displays information about users and terminals on the system.

Options:

-u   Lists only the users who are currently logged in.

-l   Lists only ports waiting for a login.

-T   Shows status of terminals.

-q   Lists only name and number of users who are logged in.

-a   Processes the */etc/utmp* file with all options turned on.

If no options are specified, **who** shows the names of the users who are currently logged in and active. It also shows the login time for these users.

Examples:

who
```
root    tty02  Nov 17 11:44
susan   tty1a  Oct  9 00:46
```

Listed here are the users who are active and logged in, as well as the terminals they are using and when they logged in.

who -u
```
root    tty02  Nov 17 11:44  0:01   79
susan   tty1a  Oct  9 00:46         166
```

The dot (.) indicates that the terminal has been active in the last minute and is "current". If the terminal has not been used in the last 24 hours, the entry is marked old. The numbers on the far right are the process ID numbers for the user's login shell.

who -T
```
root    + tty02      Nov 17   11:44
susan   - tty1a      Oct  9   00:46
```

The **-T** option displays the status of the terminal. The plus (+) character means that the terminal is writable by anyone. A minus (-) character means that the terminal has messages disabled.

who am i
```
susan   tty1a  Oct  9   00:46
```

The **am i** (or **am I**) option displays the name of the person who typed the command, in this case, susan.

See also:

date; login; whodo; whoami; ps; mesg

whoami—who am i
display user login name

whoami (or **who am i** on SCO UNIX) is a simple command that displays the user's login corresponding to the current user ID. If you have used the **su** command to temporarily log in another user, **whoami** will show the login associated with that user ID.

Command:
whoami or **who am i**

Function:
Displays the current effective user ID.

Example:

whoami
susan

whoami is a quick way to determine your current effective ID.

See also:
who; whodo.

whodo
display running programs of logged-in users

whodo shows you who is logged on the system and what programs they are running. This command produces output from the **who** and **ps** commands.

Command:
whodo

Function:
Shows what logged-in users are doing.

Example:

The information displayed depends on the security level in the system.

```
whodo
Mon Mar 14 11:43:55 1994
blueox

tty01     root       11:13
    tty01      413      0:01 sh

tty03     anne       9:18
    tty03    27161      0:01 csh
    tty03      529      0:00 sh
    tty03      535      0:00 xinit
    tty03      536      4:15 X
    tty03      538      0:00 sh
    tty03      539      0:24 scoterm
    ttyp0      543      0:01 csh
    ttyp1      626      0:01 csh
    ttyp0      580     31:18 win
```

```
     ttyp0       581       1:44 xcrt
     tty03       540       0:01 dclock
     tty03       541       0:04 mwm

ttyp0      anne       9:19

ttyp1      anne      10:03
```

whodo shows that the system adminstrator (*root*) for the system (*blueox*) is running csh. anne is running lots of applications, such as dclock and csh.

See also:

date; who; ps.

write
write a message

write sends a message directly to the screen of another user who is logged in. Users can only receive **write** messages if they have granted permission by means of the **mesg** command.

Command:
write *username* [*ttyname*]

Function:
Copies lines from your standard input to another user's screen.

Options:
ttyname   Sends message to the specified terminal if the user is logged in more than once.

Arguments:
The user's login name.

Examples:
When you invoke the **write** command, the recipient of your message receives a message that looks like the following:

```
Message from your_name on your_machine (ttyname) ...
```

After typing the command and the recipient's login, enter your message. What you type appears line-by-line on the other person's screen. You may exit the **write** program by sending an interrupt signal. **write** will display an **EOF** (end of file) or **(end of message)** on the recipient's terminal and exit.

This is a modest example of how to use the **write** command:

write thomas tty03
We've got to finish all those mashed potatoes before they go bad.
<Ctrl>d

The recipient sees the following:

```
   Message from lori on blueox (ttyp1) [ Sun Mar 20 15:59:13 ] ...
We've got to finish all those mashed potatoes before they go bad.
{end of message)
```

Two people can successfully carry on a conversation using the **write** command. The following conventional protocol is suggested: when you first write to another user, wait for him/her to **write** back before writing your message. Each person should end each message with a distinctive signal, for example, // or oo, to indicate that the other user may respond.

Here is an example of a conversation between two users. The text each user types in is in bold italics, the output each user sees is in bold:

```
        Tom's terminal:                    Lori's terminal:

write lori                        Message from tom on blueox(tty5a)
Lori, do you know what              Lori, do you know what
Scipio Africanus said to            Scipio Africanus said to
Hannibal the Carthaginian?          Hannibal the Carthaginian?
//                                  //
Message from lori on blueox(tty6a)  write tom
Nope, what did he say?              Nope, what did he say?
//                                  //
The Iberian Plateau ain't           The Iberian Plateau ain't
big enough for the two              big enough for the two
of us, elephant-boy!                of us, elephant-boy!
//                                  //
<Ctrl>d                             <Ctrl>d
(end of message)                    (end of message)
```

See also:

mail; mesg; who; talk.

Appendix A:
Shell scripts

As a user, you usually see the part of UNIX called the shell. The shell is a type of translator between you and the other parts of the UNIX operating system. Typically, you write your commands and the shell translates them into procedures that the other parts of the system can carry out. The shell also translates messages sent to you by UNIX about your command. As has been mentioned elsewhere, a number of different shells are available to users.

All UNIX systems contain a standard shell (the Bourne shell or **sh**). Other commonly used shells include C-shell (**csh**), Korn shell (**ksh**), Restricted shell (**rsh**), Visual Shell and UUCP. This appendix focuses on the Bourne shell.

In addition to interpreting commands issued at a command prompt, UNIX shells can execute several commands in sequence through the use of what are called shell scripts. **vi** (or any other ASCII text editor) can be used to create such command or shell scripts. (These files are similar to DOS "batch" files.) UNIX shell scripts are much more powerful. In addition to the traditional UNIX commands, a UNIX shell script (like many programming languages) can also contain control structures, variables and arguments. This appendix discusses how shell scripts are created

Although the syntax for the different command shells is similar, they all use different control structures, variables and arguments. This appendix covers shell scripts only for the **Bourne shell.**

C-shell should be used for interactive command scripts. C-shell accepts most of the Bourne shell syntax, but most of the control structures, e.g., conditionals like **if, for, while** or **case**, have a separate syntax. Bourne shell is the one most often used for shell scripts because it is portable across many different UNIX systems. Korn shell can also be used. Korn shell is a mixture of C shell and Bourne shell. Most Bourne shell command files are compatible with those under Korn shell. In addition, the Korn shell uses more of the syntax found under C-shell. For more information on the various shells, see the articles on each in the main body of the reference.

Simple shell scripts

The following is an example of a command script named *test*. It contains several shell commands which we could execute, one command at a time, from the system prompt:

```
:
# Cake program
food="cakes"
echo "Do you eat $food"
echo 'Do you eat $food'
```

The first line contains a : (colon). The colon indicates that this is a Bourne shell command file. The second line begins with a # . The # tells the shell not to read this line. The # is used in command files whenever you want to "comment out" (tell the shell to ignore) a line. In this case the line is used to include the name of the program in the file. However, if the file *starts* with a #, it is a C-shell command script.

The third line assigns the variable **cakes** to the text string **food**. You may, at any place in the program file, assign a variable. If you will use the variables later on, prefix the variable with a $.

The fourth and fifth lines use the command **echo**. **echo** echoes strings of text to the screen (see the article on **echo**). At the fourth line, we use the double quotation marks both at the left and the right side of a text string to insure that the content of the variable is displayed on the screen. At the fifth line, we use ' (single quotations). This insures that the string is interpreted as a string of text, but the content of the variable is not displayed at the screen.

Writing a shell script

To be able to create a command (batch) file, you have to know how to create a text file. For short shell scripts, you can use **cat**. For most shell scripts however, you should use a good ASCII editor, such as **emacs** or **vi**. Any editor you use, however, must be able to store files in pure text formats (ASCII), without any formatting codes.

Executing shell scripts

There are several ways to execute a shell script. The easiest is to have the shell do it. If you want the Bourne shell to run the *test* script we created above, enter the following command:

sh *test*

You could also redirect the standard input as follows (see Standard input, Standard output and Standard error):

sh < *test*

Still, the most common way of running a command file is to make it executable. There are lots of ways to do this. One easy one is the following:

chmod 755 *test*

This command makes *test* readable and executable for every user. However, only the file owner can alter file contents. Once a file is executable, you need only write its name for it to execute (see **chmod** for more information on file permissions).

Some simple examples

To better understand how shell scripts work, you should start with a few simple examples. What follows are a few UNIX commands. When these commands are inserted into executable files, they become simple shell scripts. The first script, sendbanner, sends a message to all the other users. To create sendbanner, insert the following lines in a file named *sendbanner*.

NOTE:

When we refer to a shell script as an executable command it is placed in bold (e.g., **sendbanner**). However, all executable commands are also files. Thus, when we refer to a shell script as a file, it is placed in italic type (e.g., *sendbanner*).

```
:
banner "Hello there" > /dev/tty5a
```

After you save the file, make the file executable by entering the following at a UNIX prompt:

chmod 755 *sendbanner*

Now, when you enter **sendbanner** at a UNIX prompt, the text string "`Hello there`" is sent to user using */dev/tty5a* (a terminal). The UNIX command **banner** prints its arguments (in this case, `Hello there`) in large letters to the standard output (usually the screen).

Let's call the second script **davidsdu**. To create **davidsdu** complete the following steps:

1. Insert the following text in a file named *davidsdu*:

   ```
   :
   banner " Utilization of disk"
   du /usr/david
   ```

2. After you save the file, make it executable by entering the command

   chmod 755 *davidsdu*

davidsdu is complete. Every time you enter **davidsdu**, the script displays a summary of the amount of disk space used by david.

Because you are now accustomed to how shell scripts work, the following simple examples will assume three things:

1. **You have inserted the command text in a script file.**
2. **The name of the file is the name you have selected for your command.**
3. **The file has been made executable.**

Each script example uses the script name as a title. It is followed by the code to be included in the script. After the code is a short description of what the script does.

sendterm
```
:
sh | tee /dev/tty5b
```

This script uses **tee** to send a picture of the present terminal to */dev/tty5b* (another terminal). To learn more about **tee**, refer to your UNIX command reference or enter **man tee** at a UNIX prompt.

sendout
```
:
cu -lttyla -s9600 dir
```

This script uses **cu** (call up) to check if the requested speed (9600 baud) is available from the serial port (*/dev/tty1a*). If it is, a connection is made to `dir`. To learn more about **cu**, refer to your UNIX command reference or enter **man cu** at a UNIX prompt.

lsort:
```
:
ls /bin | sort
```

This script lists the files in the */bin* directory and then uses **sort** to sort the output. (for more information on **ls** and **sort**, see the articles on those commands).

systemstat:
```
:
pstat | grep files
pstat | grep inode
pstat | grep processes
```

This script displays the number of open files and inodes, as well as the number of processes currently active—just the kind of information a system administrator may need!

---

fcount:
```
:
ls -l | sed 1d | wc -l
```

This script displays a list of files—one per line (**ls -l**). The rest of the command uses **sed** and **wc** to display the number of files (**sed 1d | wc -l**). For more information about **sed** or **wc** refer to your UNIX command reference or enter **man sed** or **man wc** at a UNIX prompt.

Variables used by the shell

All UNIX variables are memory locations used to store data. Because they are "variables", they are objects that can take any one of a set of values. However, all variables have a second level. The second level is defined by use.

Shell variables are variables defined by a given shell for use only by that shell. Shell variables are memory locations used to store values used by a shell.

Environment variables are shell variables that are part of a given user's environment. **Environment variables** create an environment that is accessible to all shells. As such, they can be accessed by any shell started by a user or by a program started by that user. Environment variables are usually used to provide data that commands need in order to execute.

Shell variables

Here are a few examples of shell variables:

- **computer=Zenith386**
- **number=3.14**
- **food=cheese**
- **price=12**
- **directory=/usr/david/c-files**
- **homedirectory='pwd'**

A shell variable can have a null value. In the following the variable, **percentage** is set to null or zero:

percentage=

Using shell variables

To use a shell variable prefix it with the dollar sign (**$**). For example, to discover the content of a variable use the command
echo $ *variablename*

Thus, if the shell variable **directory** was defined as */u/kentd/work/Hegelbook*, the command
cp *article.apsa* **$directory**
copies the file *article.apsa* to */u/kentd/work/Hegelbook*.
To define a variable that uses a command or control character, enclose it in single quotes. For example,
todaysdate='date'
user='who | wc -l'

Similarly, if a variable contains an apostrophe, it must be enclosed with double quotes. For example,
text="Several PC's are sold"

Lastly, if a variable contains quotation marks it must be enclosed with a second set of double quotations. For example,
text=""Hello there""

Environment variables (System variables)

Environment variables are always written with capital letters. They are used to define important parts of a user's working environment. For example, the Bourne shell recognizes the environment variable **PATH. PATH** defines where all shells (started after **PATH** is defined) look for executable commands.

PATH defines the search path for commands. If you do not define a search **PATH**, your commands are executed only if they reside in the current working directory.

Using environment variables
Environment variables are used in the same way as shell variables. For example, to display the contents of **$HOME** (an environment variable), issue the following command
$echo $HOME
This command displays the path name of your home directory.

Common shell environment variables:

For a discussion of the most common Bourne shell, C-shell and Korn shell environment variables, see the articles under those headings.

UNIX command position definitions

The shell divides commands into commands and arguments (options are a type of argument to a command). When a command is executed, the shell creates a variable for each position. **$0** contains the name of the command. **$1** is the first argument, **$2** the second, and so on up to **$9**.

If you start a shell script with one argument, the name of the script takes position **$0**, and the argument becomes **$1**. If you have different arguments each time you run the script, the content of **$1** will be different.

Examples:

start a b c d
Here, **start** is **$0**, **a** is **$1**, **b** is **$2**, **c** is **$3** and **d** is **$4**.$

You may also assign the position values directly using **set**. For example,
set Hegel right was after all
Here $1 is assigned to the text string **Hegel**, $2 to the text string **right**, $3 to the text string **was**, $4 to the text string **after**, and $5 to the text string **all**. If you then enter the command
echo "$1, $3, $2, $4, $5"
your screen would display:

```
Hegel was right after all
```

Predefined variables

The shell also uses several other predefined variables. These may be included in shell scripts to construct various control structure tests. For example,

$#	Displays the number of arguments included in a command line. For example, **test A B C, $#** displays the result: 3
$?	Displays status of the last command executed. If the command was free of syntax errors the value is set to zero.
$n	The argument of the command. May have values from 1 to n
$*	Displays all the arguments
$$	Displays the process number of the current process
$!	Displays the process number of the last background process.
$-	Displays a list of execution flags used.

Examples:

The following simple examples assume three things:
1.   **You have inserted the command text in a script file.**
2.   **The name of the file is the name you have selected for your command.**
3.   **The file has been made executable.**
Each script example uses the script name as a title. It is followed by the code to be included in the script. After the code is a short description of what the script does.

1. **number**:
```
:
echo $#
```
number uses : to indicate that this is a Bourne shell script. The character $# displays the number of arguments. Run **number**, using the arguments **a**, **b**, **c** and **d**. For example,
number a b c d
displays

4

$0 is now the name of the command (number). **$1** is a, **$2** is b, etc. **$1** to **$9** varies each time **number** is run.

2. where:
```
:
who | grep $1
```
The following command
where jane
displays the tty numbers that **jane** is using (assuming she is logged in).

3. variable:
```
:
echo Number of arguments is $#.
date &
echo Process id from the date-command was $!.
wait
echo Process id for this shell is $$.
grep vt100 /etc/ttytype
echo The return code from grep was $?.
echo We had the following set options $-.
```

This script uses all the predefined variables. Note that no double quotation marks are used. If you use **echo** with double quotes, the result will be the same. That is, `echo The number of arguments is $#` is the same as `echo "Number of arguments is $#."`.

The following
sh -x variable A B > testfile
creates **testfile** with the following content:

```
+ :
+ Number of arguments is 2.
+ date
+ echo Process id from the date-command was 1293.
+ wait
+ echo Process id for this shell is 1292.
+ grep vt100 /etc/ttytype
+ echo The return-code from grep was 1.
+ echo We had the following set of options x.
```

UNIX commands by example

Creating variables with read

With help of the **read** command, we can create an interactive variable. If you use **read** in a shell script, the shell reads from the default input and places the input into a variable.

For example,

```
:
clear
echo "Hello!"
echo "What is your name? "
read answer
echo "Fine to meet you $answer"
```

In this example, the shell reads input from a user into the variable, **answer**, and then uses **echo** to display **answer**.

If you want to have a larger number of terminal codes, use the command **tput**. For more information on **echo** and **tput**, see their respective articles.

NOTE:

If you are using the command **echo**, separate the argument with a space and terminate the argument with a line feed. **echo** also accepts the following special codes:

\b	one character to the left (backspace)
\c	print line without line feed
\f	new page (form feed)
\r	return (carriage return)
\v	vertical tab
\t	horizontal tab
\\n	echoes an ASCII character whose octal code is n

Examples:

1. **info:**
```
:
echo "Today's date and time          :   \c"
date
echo "Number of users                :   \c"
who | wc -l
echo "My personal status             :   \c"
who am i
```
info displays today's date and time, number of users and your personal status. Text is first displayed at the screen with the command **echo**. The code \c prohibits line feed. The result of **date** is placed on the same line.

2. **info1**
```
:
TIME="Today's date and time          :   \c"
USER="Number of users                :   \c"
ME="Personal status                  :   \c"
echo "$TIME"
date
echo "$USER"
who | wc -l
echo "$ME"
who am I
```
info1 defines three text variables which are displayed by **echo**. The output of **echo1** is the same as **info**.

UNIX commands by example

Conditional commands

The UNIX programming language has logical control structures. This section examines the most important ones. The syntax is based on Bourne shell conventions. In C shell the principles are similar, but the syntax is somewhat different. For more information on C-shell programming, refer to a C-shell command reference.

Shell scripts often make use of looped command arguments. Such arguments repeat or "loop" executing conditional commands for each argument. The Bourne shell has several effective aids for controlling loop flow i.e., **for**, **if**, **case** and **while**

These commands can either be entered at a shell prompt, or run in a shell script.

Using "for"

The **for** command can perform multiple operations on a given file, or it can execute a command with several arguments. The general syntax for a **for** loop is:

```
for variable in word-list
do
command-list
done
```

`word-list` is a list of variables separated by blanks. `command-list` is executed once for each word in `word-list`.

Examples:

printoutnumber
```
:
for i in `ls`
do
pr -f $i ;
done
```
printoutnumber prints all the files in the current directory. A word list is generated by the **ls** command. **ls** generates a list of the files in the current working directory. Each single file is placed in **$i**, formatted by the **pr** command and sent to the printer.

If a `word-list` is not created, you can use the same command for all the arguments. **checkif** provides a simple example.

checkif:
```
:
for i
do grep $i *.c
done
```
Once you have created **checkif**, try,
checkif `hash(`insert`
checkif checks all C-program files (those ending with .c) in the current directory for the text string "hash(`insert".

Using "case"

case, makes it possible to jump to various locations in a shell program. The general syntax is:

```
case word in
pattern1) commandlist1;;
pattern2) commandlist2;;
...
esac
```

When using **case**, the shell script compares **word** against all the patterns in the **case** statement. If it finds a **word** in **pattern1**, **commandlist1** is executed. If **word** is found in **pattern2**, **commandlist2** is executed etc. If **word** is not found, no commands are executed.

;;	terminates a case loop
;;	terminates each command list.
esac	marks the end of the case block

Examples:

choice:
:
```
case $1 in
        1) who;;
        2) whodo;;
        3) who am i;;
        0) exit;;
esac
```
Here the case loop uses the first position parameter (**$1**) as a variable. Once you have created **choice**, if you enter
case choice 3
the command, **who am i,** is executed.

Using "if"

The shell provides a structured conditional capability with **if**. The simplest **if** command has the following syntax:

```
if command list
then command list
fi
```

Once the condition `command` or `command list` is satisfied, then a second `command list` is executed. In most cases, **if** is used as a test. If the result is true (0=true), the command or list of commands following **then** is executed. **fi** signifies the end of the **if** test. To execute commands if the **if** test is false, use **else**. For example,

```
if command list
then command list
else command list
fi
```

Examples:

checkpass *username*

```
:
for i
do
      if grep $i /etc/passwd
      then
            echo "$i is defined in /etc/passwd"
      else
            echo "$i is not defined in /etc/passwd"
      fi
done
```

checkpass looks in */etc/passwd* for the **username** specified in argument number one. If it is present, **checkpass** echoes one of two lines of text. For example, if karlmarx was a user on your system, the following command

checkpass karlmarx

would display output resembling the following:

```
karlmarx:*:200:100:revolutionist:/usr/karlmarx:/bin/csh
karlmarx is defined in /etc/passwd
```

passgroup provides a more complex example.

passgroup

```
:
BB=/dev/null
for NAME in $@; do
      if grep $NAME /etc/passwd > $BB 2>$BB; then
            echo $NAME is found in file password
      else
            if grep $NAME /etc/group >$BB 2>$BB; then
                        echo $NAME is found in file group
            else
                        echo $NAME is either found in
                        echo file password or group
            fi
      fi
done
```

passgroup requires *username* as an argument. If *username* is found in
/etc/passwd or */etc/group*, **passgroup** displays a message. Note that **BB** is equated
to */dev/null*. This means that **BB** sends data to an dead-end device. "**if**" structures
are used to find out if *username* exists in */etc/passwd*, */etc/group* or in both files.
The message displayed varies depending on the result of the **if** command.

Using the "while" loop

while uses the following syntax:

```
while commandlist1
do
       commandlist2
done
```

The commands in `commandlist2` are executed as long as `commandlist1` is
true (status=1). If the exit status of the last command in the `commandlist1` is false
(status=0), then the commands in the second command list (command list2) are not
executed. `commandlist2` is repeated as long as the exit status of `commandlist1`
is true (status=1). A **while** loop is executed only as long as `commandlist1` returns
a non zero exit status.

Examples:

readable
```
:
while test -r *
do
     ls -la *
done
```
If a file is readable (for more information on **test** see "Using the test command")
readable lists it.

```
copypair
:
while test "$2" != ""; do
    cp $1 $2
    shift; shift
done
if test "$1" != ""; then
    echo "$0: unequal number of arguments!"
fi
```
copypair copies pairs of files. (This shell script uses the shell command **shift.**
For more information on **shift**, see "Position parameters and the shift command") .
If you enter
copypair *file1 file2 file3 file4*
copypair copies *file1* to *file2*, *file3* to *file4*.

Using the "until" loop

If **while** loops as long as `commandlist` (or the condition) is true (status=0),
until loops as long as `commandlist` (or the condition) is false.

Example:

```
untiltest
:
until test -f datafile
do
    sleep 1000
done
```
untiltest goes in a loop until *datafile* is created. **untiltest** tests for *datafile* every
1000 units of time (about 500 seconds).

UNIX commands by example

Using the "test" command

test returns an initial status. This status is used with conditional commands. **test** is only used in shell scripts For example, the command

test -f file

returns the initial status zero (true) if the file exists, and an initial status (false) if the file does not exist. **test** accepts the following arguments:

test -s *file*	True if *file* exists and is not empty.
test -f *file*	True if *file* exists and is a normal *file*.
test -r *file*	True if *file* is readable.
test -w *file*	True if *file* is writable.
test -x *file*	True if *file* exists and is executable.
test -d *file*	True if *file* is a directory.
test -n s1	True if length of the string (**s1**) is not zero.
test -z s1	True if length of the string (**s1**) is equal to zero.
test string1 = string2	True if **string1** and **string2** are equal.
test string1! = string2	True if **string1** and **string2** are unequal.
test string1	True if **string1** is not a null string.
test n1 -eq n2	True if integers **n1** and **n2** are equal.
test n1 -ne n2	True if integers **n1** and **n2** are unequal.
test n1 -gt n2	True if integer **n1** is greater than **n2**.
test n1 -ge n2	True if integer **n1** is greater than or equal to **n2**.
test n1 -lt n2	True if integer **n1** is less than **n2**.
test n1 -le n2	True if integer **n1** is less than or equal to **n2**..

Example:

test can be combined with other operators, For example,

checkpass:
```
:
if test $# = 0
then echo "You have to write a user name!"
else grep $1 /etc/passwd
fi
```
checkpass checks to see if any arguments are specified. If no arguments are specified, **echo** sends "You have to write a user name" to the screen. If an argument is specified, **checkpass** searches (**grep**) for it in */etc/passwd*.

Position parameters and the "shift" command

When a shell script starts, the shell automatically creates "position parameters". The shell script itself is **$0**, the first argument is **$1**, the next **$2** and so on up to **$9**. Shell scripts are limited to nine position parameters.

shift overcomes this limitation by "shifting" command arguments one position to the left. When **shift** is used, the original value of **$1**, is discarded. **$1** receives the value of **$2**, **$2** gets the value of **$3** and so on.

Examples:

echoshift
```
:
while test $#!=0
do
     echo $1 $2 $3 $4 $5 $6 $7 $8 $9
     shift
done
```
while **test** is true, i.e., as long it hasn't run out of arguments, **echoshift** echoes the value of the arguments. **shift** moves the original arguments one position to the left until it runs out of arguments. Each time we loop, we also move to the left. For example, if you issue the following command
echoshift a b c
you would see the following:

```
a b c
b c
c
```

Here's another example:
namecount
```
:
countvar=1
while test $countvar -le 12
do
     echo "name : $1"
     shift
done
```
This command can be used to read up to twelve names.

Using "break" and "continue"

break allows you to exit from a **for** or **while** loop. **break** *n* allows you to exit from *n* levels of a **for** or **while** loop. The default is one level. If you want to skip the rest of the current **for** or **while** loop and resume execution with the next iteration of the loop, use the command **continue**. Both **break** and **continue** are used between the commands **do** and **done**.

Example:

```
:
while true
do
      echo "Enter data"
      read indata
      case "$indata" in
      "done")    break
           ;;
      "")
           continue
           ;;
      *)
           echo "Hello"
           ;;
      esac
done
```

while true is a continuous loop. If you enter the text **break**, the program exits the loop structure. If you press **<Enter>**, only, the program jumps to the beginning of the loop and **indata** is read again. If you enter your name (or anything else), the text **Hello** is displayed.

Using the "exit" command

exit sends positive or negative status messages. The status value 0 (zero) is given after an error free execution of a command. Otherwise, the status value takes on a value between 1 and 3.

exit codes are used to communicate between shells. **exit** simulates the termination of a command. A command file can be terminated normally by placing **exit** 0 as the last statement in the file.

Exit code description:

Code	meaning
0	command succeeds
1	command fails
2	syntax error
3	does not catch the interrupt signal

Example:

```
if test $# -lt 2
then
    echo "We need two or more arguments";exit 0
fi
```

This section of shell script tests the number of arguments the user has written. If the user has specified less than two arguments, the program exits.

The following shell script section returns either a positive (0) or negative (1) message.

```
if grep $var orderlist
then
    exit 0
else
    echo "Was not inside the orderlist"
    exit 1
fi
```

Grouping commands

Within a shell, you can group commands two different ways:

- With parentheses ( ). Parentheses create a sub shell that reads the commands included in the parentheses. The left and right parentheses can be placed anywhere in a line.

- With curly brackets { }. Curly brackets do not create a sub-shell. The commands are read directly from the shell. Curly brackets are commonly used when the default output of one set of commands is used as default input to another command. Curly brackets are only accepted if the left bracket (e. g. {) is the first character of the command line.

UNIX commands by example

Examples:

(date; who | wc -l) >> *datafile*
First, **date** is executed. Then **wc** counts the number of users logged on to the system (**who | wc -l**). The results of both commands are appended to *datafile*.

(cc -o *calc calc.c*; **strip** *calc*; **mv** *calc calculate*) **&**
cc compiles the C program *calc.c* and creates the compiled binary *calc*. It then strips *calc* and changes its name to *calculate*. All the operations are executed in the background.

Parentheses can make executing commands in another directory easier. For example, the following two sets of commands achieve the same result:

directory='pwd'; cd /etc/conf/cf.d
./link_unix; cd $directory
and
(cd /etc/conf/cf.d; ./link_unix)

In both cases, the UNIX kernel is relinked. However, in the second example, we create a sub-shell and therefore never leave the current working directory.

{ls */dev*; **ls** */dev/dsk*} **| tr [a-z] [A-Z]**
In this example, all the files in */dev* and */dev/dsk* become default input to the **tr** command.

Commands in variables

The output from any command can be assigned to a variable. This is called command substitution. To replace a command with its output, assign a variable name to the command enclosed in single quotation marks. (The command must be surrounded by single quotes).

> **Example:**
>
> **todaysdate='date'**
> The output from the **date** command is placed in the shell variable **todaysdate**. To display **todaysdate**, enter
> **echo $todaysdate**
>
> You can also substitute a variable for the output from a series of commands. For example,
>
> **numberofiles='ls | wc -l'**
> Here **numberofiles** is the number produced by the command sequence **'ls | wc -l'**

Reserved characters in shell script commands and expressions

The following is a list of the most common symbols, wildcards and reserved words used in shell scripts. Some new reserved words are introduced. In addition, see the discussion in "Redirection" and "Pipes and filters".

Metacharacters

|	Pipe symbol.
&&	(and if symbol). If you write two commands with **&&** in between them, the last command is executed only if the first is terminated after a successful execution.
||	(or-if symbol). If you write two commands with || between them, the last command is executed only if the first was terminated after a non-successful execution.
;	Separates commands.
;;	Terminates a case condition.
&	Processes an operation in background.
(...)	Groups commands using sub shells.
<	Redirects default input.
<<	Here document (see "Using "here" documents").
>	Redirects default output.

>>	Adds to default output.
#	If a line in a shell script begins with a # (pound sign or cross hatch), the shell does not read the line. This is usually used to include explanatory comments inside the shell script.

Patterns (Wild cards)

*	Replaces one or several characters.
?	Replaces one character.
[...]	Matches any of enclosed characters.

Reserved words

if	esac
then	for
else	while
elif	until
fi	do
case	done
in	{ }

See also:

Files; Redirection; Pipes and filters. Information about variables is found throughout this appendix.

Using "here" documents

The << [-] *name* command reads input on a secondary shell until *name* is found. This is called a "here document". Basically, it means that the shell should read the data from the file until "here" which is designated by *name*.

Example:

```
for i
do
grep $i <<STOP
        123.45     Oslo
        124.50     Copenhagen
        156.60     Stockholm
        124.56     Helsinki
        125.76 London
        STOP
done
```
The shell uses the text between **<<STOP** and **STOP** as standard input for the **grep** command. This example uses **STOP** as the stop *name*. If the hyphen is used, all initial tab characters are removed from input lines.

See also:
Redirection; Pipes and filters.

Functions and procedures

Most programming languages collect declarations and statements that perform specific tasks into functions. Bourne shell scripts use functions in the same manner as other programming languages This allows you to define procedures that may be used many times in a given shell script.

The basic syntax of shell functions is:

```
name ()
{
command list;
}
```

UNIX commands by example

Examples:

The following defines the function, standard_text.

```
standard_text ()
{
echo "***********************************************"
echo "           Prentice Hall       "
echo "***********************************************"
}
```

To call this function, write the name of the function. In this case, the name is
standard_text.

This following reads text and determines if you have written yes or no.

```
fetch_yes_no ()
    while echo "$* (y/n)? \C" >& 2
    do
            read yes_no
            case $yes_no in
            [yY]) return 0;;
            [nN]) return 1;;
            *)    echo "Answer yes or no" >& 2;;
            esac
    done
}
```

This function adds the text (y/n) to the default output. The function only accepts Y,
y, N, n as input, and returns a code 0 or 1. If the input from the user is anything else,
the function sends the text "Answer yes or no". It loops forever if the user does
not answer Y, y, N or n.

Procedures

A procedure is a separate executable shell script. Once created, a procedure can
be called from the main shell script.

Remember that the main program and all related procedures should be placed in
the same directory. If they are not, your path must include the location of the
procedure.

> ## Example:
>
> First, create a procedure named **letter_to_all**.
>
> **letter_to_all**
>
> ```
> letter=$1
> shift
> for i in $*
> do mail $i < $letter
> done
> ```
> Once you make this procedure executable, it can be called from any other shell
> script. For example,
> **letter_to_all report david john peter**

Using "set" to set options

It is often useful to change the shell's execution options. You can use **set** to
activate (-) or deactivate (+) flags that affect the operation of the active shell, to
display the names and content of shell variables, and to display the names and
definition of current functions.

Syntax:

set   [-/+ aefknuvx]

Using + rather than - causes these flags to be turned off. These flags can also be
used when starting the shell. The current set of flags is stored in the shell variable $-
. The remaining arguments are position parameters and are assigned, in order, to $1,
$2, etc. If no arguments are given, the values of all names are printed.

Options:

-/+a	Export (don't export) variables which are created or modified.
-/+e	Exits (or doesn't exit) if a command exits with a non zero exit status.
-/+f	Disables (or enables) filename generation.

-/+k	Places (does not place) all keyword arguments (shell variables) in the environment for a command.
-/+n	Reads commands but does not execute (or reads and executes) them.
-/+u	Treats (does not treat) unset variables as an error when attempting a substitution.
-/+v	Displays (or does not display) input lines as fast as they are read by the shell. This option is commonly used to isolate errors in shell scripts.
-/+x	Displays (or does not display) commands and their arguments after they are ready for execution. Although this flag is passed to subshells, it does not enable tracing in those subshells.
--	Does not change any of the flags; useful in setting **$1** to ``-".

Shell program example

The following is an example of a relatively complex shell script. It creates a menu system that gives users easy access to a number of UNIX tools. You may modify this file according to your needs. The example uses most of the commands found in this chapter. If you enter the text by hand, take care to enter the syntax exactly as presented.

```
:
clear
while test "$ans" != "0"
do
clear
echo ""
echo "                    *      FUNCTIONS    *"
echo "                    ---------------------    "
echo "              1 - Lists files/directories"
```

```
echo "                  2 - Change directory        "
echo "                  3 - Check file        "
echo "                  4 - Copy file"
echo "                  5 - Remove file        "
echo "                  6 - Change name of file     "
echo "                  7 - Display file to screen"
echo "                  8 - Print file to printer "
echo "                  9 - Logged/on active users"
echo "                  10 - Who am i          "
echo "                  11 - Current directory     "
echo "                  12 - Create a subdirectory "
echo "                  13 - Remove a subdirectory "
echo "                  14 - Exit menusystem        "
echo ""
echo "              Choose function (1/../14) and press the <CR>
key: \c" read ans
#  cd $home
#      1 - List files/directories
if test "$ans" = "1";then
      clear
      echo ""
      echo " Current directory is : \c"
      pwd
      echo ""
      echo " View of files/directories "
      ls -la | more
      echo ""
      echo " Press <CR> to go on : \c "
      read stop
fi
#      2 - Change directory
if test "$ans" = "2";then
      clear
      echo ""
      echo " Current directory is : \c"
      pwd
      echo ""
      echo " Proceed in current directory, answer with
'.'(dot)and press <CR>"
      echo " To step up one level, answer with '..'(2-dot)
and press <CR>"
      echo ""
```

```
        echo " To go to the home directory, answer with <CR>"
        echo ""
        echo " To go to the sub/directory under current
directory,"
        echo " Write the name of sub/directory and press
<RETURN>"
        echo ""
        echo " Which directory do you want to use : \c"
        read directory
        cd $directory
        echo ""
        echo " New current directory is : \c"
        pwd
        echo ""
        echo " Press <CR> to go on : \c"
        read stop
fi
#       3 - Check file

if test "$ans" = "3";then
        clear
        echo ""
        echo " Which file do you wish to check : \c"
        read filec
        if test -d "$filec";then
                echo ""
                echo "    "$filec" is a directory"
                echo ""
                echo "    Press <CR> to go on : \c"
                read stop
        fi
        if test -r "$filec";then
                echo ""
                echo "    File is readable"
        fi
        if test -w "$filec";then
                echo ""
                echo "    File may be written to"
        fi
        if test ! -f "$filec";then
                echo ""
```

```
        echo "   "$filec" is neither a directory nor a file in
current directory" fi
        echo ""
        echo " Press <CR> to go on : \c"
        read stop
fi
#       4 - Copy file
if test "$ans" = "4";then
        clear
        echo ""
        echo ""
        echo " You are now using directory : \c"
        pwd
        echo ""
        echo " Which file do you wish to copy : \c"
        read sourcefile
        echo ""
        if test  -s "$sourcefile";then
echo "   Which directory/file do you wish to copy to : \c"
                read targetfile
                if test ! -s "$targetfile";then
                          cp "$sourcefile" "$targetfile"
                else
                    echo ""
echo "   "$targetfile" exist, do you want to overwrite (y/n):
\c" read yes
                    if test "$yes" = "y";then
                          cp "$sourcefile" "$targetfile"
                    fi
                fi
        else
              echo ""
echo "   "$sourcefile" does not exist - press <CR> : \c"
              read stop
        fi
fi
#       5 - Remove file
if test "$ans" = "5";then
        clear
        echo ""
              echo "   Which file do you wish to remove : \c"
              read file
              if test -f "$file";then
```

```
                    clear
                    echo ""
echo "   "$file" exist. Do you really wish to remove it (y/n):
\c" read yes
                    if test "$yes" = "y";then
                              rm $file
                    fi
        else echo ""
echo "   "$file" does not exist - press <CR> : \c"
                         read stop
              fi
fi
#      6 - Change name of file
if test "$ans" = "6";then
              clear
              echo ""
              echo "   You are now in directory : \c"
              pwd
              echo ""
              echo "   Which file is going to be renamed  :
\c"
              read file
              if test -f "$file";then
                    clear
                    echo ""
                    echo "   "$file" exists. Give it a new name
: \c"
                    read newname
                    if test ! -f "$newname";then
                              mv "$file" "$newname"
                    else
                              echo ""
                              echo "   "$newname" exist -
press <CR> : \c"
                              read stop
                    fi
              else
                    echo ""
echo "    "$file" does not exist / press <CR> : \c"
                    read stop
              fi
fi
```

```
#               7 - Display file
if test "$ans" = "7";then
         clear
         echo ""
echo "    If the content is displayed over more than one"
         echo "   screen/full, press <CR> to go on."
         echo ""
         echo "    Which file should be displayed : \c"
         read file
         echo ""
         echo ""
         echo " Press <CR>."
         if test  -s "$file";then
                pr -125 -p "$file"
                echo ""
                echo " Press CR> to go one : \c"
                read stop
         else
                echo ""
                echo "    The file does not exist or is
emty."
                echo ""
                echo "   Press <CR> to go on : \c"
                read stop
         fi
fi
#               8 - Print file
if test "$ans" = "8";then
         clear
         echo ""
echo "    Which file is going to be printed? :\c " read fil
         echo ""
         lpr $fil
         echo ""
fi
#         9  - Logged-on/active users on the system
if test "$ans" = "9";then
      clear
      echo ""
      echo "      Checks,wait.....\c"
             who > /tmp/who-list
             clear
```

```
                echo ""
                echo "Users logged-on : "
                echo ""
        cat /tmp/who-list
        echo ""
                echo "Total logged-on : \c"
        cat /tmp/who-list | wc -1
        echo ""
                echo "Press <CR> to go on: \c "
                read stop
fi
#       10 - Who am i
if test "$ans" = "10";then
                clear
                echo ""
                echo "I am : \c"
                who am i
                echo ""
                echo "Press <CR> to go on : \c"
                read stop
fi
#       11 - Current directory
if test "$ans" = "11";then
                clear
                echo ""
                echo "       Current directory :\c"
                pwd
                echo ""
                echo "       Press <CR> to go on :\c"
                read stop
fi
#      12 - Create a subdirectory
if test "$ans" = "12";then
                clear
                echo ""
                echo "   Current directory is : \c"
                pwd
                echo "  "
echo " Is this the correct directory / do you wish to go on
(y/n) : \c" read yes
                if test "$yes" = "y";then
                        echo ""
```

```
echo "  What is the name of the new subdirectory : \c" read
subdir
                if test ! -d  "$subdir";then
                        mkdir "$subdir"
                        if test ! -d "$subdir";then
                                echo ""
                                echo "   "$subdir" is not
created : \c"
                                read stop
                        fi
                else
                        echo ""
echo "   "$subdir" already exists - press <CR> " read stop
                fi
        fi
fi
#       13 - Remove emty subdirectory
if test "$ans" = "13";then
        clear
        echo ""
        echo "Current directory is : \c"
        pwd
        echo ""
echo "Which subdirectory do you wish to remove : \c" read
removedir
        if test  -d "$removedir";then
                cd $removedir
                echo ""
echo "Control of directory - Answer = \c"
                ls
                cd    ..
                echo ""
echo "Is answer = total 0 - (y/n) : \c"
                read yes
                if test "$yes" = "y";then
                        rmdir "$removedir"
                        if test ! -d "$removedir";then
                                echo ""
echo ""$removedir" is removed - <CR> : \c" read stop
                        fi
                fi
        else
```

```
                    echo ""
echo ""$removedir" is not a directory <CR> : \c" read stop
            fi
fi

#          14 - Exit menusystem
if test "$ans" = "14";then
      exit;
fi
done
```

Appendix B
Editing text with vi

vi is able to write, correct and edit text , script (batch) or program files. **vi** commands can be divided into three groups or modes: Full-screen mode, Insert mode and Command mode.

Full-screen mode

When starting **vi**, you will always enter full screen mode. If you are unsure of which mode you are in, press **<Esc>**. Esc will always bring you back to full screen mode.

In full screen mode, you can move around in the document, search for words and replace words. You may also store a document or terminate vi. For a list of all the full screen mode commands, see the "Command" sections later in this appendix.

In full screen mode, to exit **vi** saving the current file, enter **ZZ.**

Insert or text mode

To be able to write text or to make changes in a file, you have to be in insert mode. Insert mode is sometimes called text or write mode. You can move from full screen mode to text mode using the following commands:

a	Append after cursor.
A	Append at end of line.
i	Insert before cursor.
I	Insert at the beginning of the line.
o	Open for editing the line below.
O	Open for editing the line above.
rx	Replace character under the cursor with character x.
R	Overstrike characters beginning with character under the cursor.
~	Change lower case to upper case and vice-versa.

Command mode

Enter command mode by pressing : (colon) while in full screen mode. A colon (:) appears in the lower left hand corner of your screen indicating that you are in command mode. In command mode, you can issue the following commands:

x	Updates file and exit **vi**.
q	Quits **vi** . **vi** displays a warning message if the file has changed since the last **w** command..
q!	Quits **vi**. Discard any changes.
e *filename*	Edits *filename*. Current file becomes alternate.
e!	Restores last saved version of the current file.
n	Edits next file. Presupposes that you are editing a list of files.
n!	Edits next file and abandons changes to current file
r *filename*	Inserts contents of ***filename*** at the cursor position before entering command mode.
w	Writes current file saving changes.
w *filename*	Writes current file to ***filename***.
w!	Forces overwrite of existing file.
wq	Writes the file and quits **vi**.

Sample vi session:

To start **vi** enter **vi** *filename*. To create a file named *text1* enter the command
vi *text1*
Starts **vi** with *text1* as an argument. An empty screen appears with the ~ character on the left side of the screen.

Start insert mode by entering **i**. Enter new text. For the purposes of this example, write

```
UNIX includes the text editor vi.....
```

To store the file and to terminate **vi**, complete the following steps:
1.   Exit insert mode by pressing **<Esc>**.
2.   Terminate **vi** by pressing **ZZ** (remember capital **Z**)

The file is stored under the name *text1* and vi is terminated.

A quick tour through vi

Each of the following sections explains in greater detail some facet of using **vi**. If you have never used **vi** before we recommend that you take a look at all of them. After you are more familiar with **vi,** use them as a reverence.

Starting vi

vi may be started in several different ways.

Command:

vi [*option*] [*filename*]

Function:

Start the text editor **vi.**

Options:

Options available on the **vi** command line include:

-c *command*   Begins editing by executing the specified editor ***command*** (usually a search or positioning command).

-r *file*   (recover). Used to recover the last saved version of a file after an editor or system crash.

-L   Lists the names of all files saved as a result of an editor or system crash. Files may be recovered with the -r option.

-w*n*   Sets the default window size to n. Useful is you have to start in small windows.

-R   Sets a read-only option so that files can be viewed but not edited.

Arguments:

Name of the file to be created or edited. Without any options or arguments, **vi** opens a new document.

Examples:

vi *letterPeter*
Opens the file *letterPeter*. If no file exists with this name, **vi** creates one when any text is saved.

vi +20 *note1*
Opens *note1* for editing and places the cursor at line number 20.

vi + *note2*
Opens *note2* for editing and places the cursor at the last line.

vi +/food *note3*
Opens *note3* for editing. Places the cursor at the first line containing the word food.

vi -r *note4*
Opens *note4* for editing. The **-r** option recovers the last saved version after a system crash or power failure

Moving around in a file

There are 4 groups of commands for moving the cursor:

1. Commands for line positioning.
2. Commands for character positioning.
3. Commands for words, sentences and paragraphs.
4. Commands to move to different file positions.

Commands for line positioning
While in full screen mode, the following commands move the cursor to the designated line.

H	top line on screen
L	last line on screen
M	middle line on screen
+	next line at first character
-	previous line at first character
CR	return, same as +
↓ or j	next line, same column
↑ or k	previous line, same column

Commands for character positioning
While in full screen mode, the following commands move the cursor to the designated character.

0	beginning of line
$	end of line
l	forward one character
h	backward one character
^H	same as backspace (^ is the same as the Ctrl key)
space bar	forward one character
f*x*	find next character *x*
F*x*	previous character *x*
t*x*	move to character prior to next character *x*
T*x*	move to character following previous character *x*

Moving the cursor by word, sentence and paragraphs
While in full screen mode, the following commands move the cursor to the designated spot.

w	forward one word
b	backward one word
e	move to the end of a word
)	move to next sentence
}	move to next paragraph
(	move backward one sentence
{	move backward one paragraph

Moving to different file positions

While in full screen mode, the following commands move the cursor to the designated position.

^F	move forward one screen (^ is the same as the Ctrl key)
^B	move backward one screen
^D	scroll down one half screen
^U	scroll up one half screen
_n_G	go to the beginning of the specified line (end default), where _n_ is a line number. G alone takes you to the end of the file.
/pat	search forward for a line containing pat
?pat	search backward for a line containing pat
x	repeat last / or ? command
N	reverse last / or ? command
]]	next section/function
[[	previous section/function

Adjusting the screen

While in full screen mode, the following commands adjust the designated aspects of the screen.

^L	clear screen and redraw window
^R	alternate clear screen and redraw window
zCR	redraw screen with current line at top of window
z-	redraw screen with current line at bottom of window
z.	redraw screen with current line at center of window
/pat/z-CR	find the next line containing pat and move it to the bottom of the window
z_n_.	use _n_ number of lines for the window
^E	scroll window down 1 line
^Y	scroll window up 1 line

Yank and put - using buffers to move text

To use **yank** and **put**, you must be in full screen mode. The following commands move text to a memory buffer (**yank**) and insert the text at another location (**put**).

4yy	**yank** 4 lines to the default buffer
4yl	**yank** 3 characters to the default buffer
p	**put** (insert) text from the default buffer after the cursor position
P	**put** (insert) text from the default buffer before the cursor position

You can also **yank** and put to named memory buffers. For example:

"*x*y	**yank** text to buffer *x*
"*x*p	**put** text from buffer *x*
"*x*d	**delete** text into buffer *x*

Defining blocks of text

If you want to do anything with blocks of text in **vi** you have to mark them. To mark a block of text, in full screen mode move the cursor to the top line in the target text and type the following:

ma

(or **m**ark point **a**). Now move the cursor to the last line of the target text block and type the following:

mb

(or **m**ark point **b**). The text between marks a and b can be manipulated from command mode using the following:

'a,'b *editaction*

where *editaction* is something you want to do the block of text between points a and b (e.g. move, copy, move to buffer or delete). For example, to move a block of text, first define the text block using the mark command. Then, move the cursor to the line above the target location and enter (from command mode):

'a,'b mo.

The period indicates that you want the text moved to the line following the cursor location. Copying the block works the same way. First define the text, then move the cursor to line above the target location and enter (from command mode):

'a,'b co.

To delete a block of text, define the text using the mark commands and then enter (from command mode):

'a,'b d

(no period is necessary as you are not moving the text). The text is deleted to the default screen buffer. If you change you mind after deleting the block of text, either enter

u

to undelete the last deletion to its original location. To insert the deleted text at a new location, move the cursor to the line above the target position and press

p

You can also combine the block commands with the yank commands. To **yank** a defined block of text to the named buffer **a,** first define the block using the **mark** command, and then enter (from command mode):

'a,'b y a

Many of these commands can be included in **vi** macros (or mapped keystrokes). See the section on **vi** macros below for more information.

Deleting text

While in full screen mode, place the cursor either on the first line you want to delete or on the first character you want to delete. Then use the following commands:

x	deletes the character under the cursor
2x	deletes the character under the cursor plus the next character to the right
xxxx	deletes the character under the cursor plus three characters to the left
dw	deletes the word following the cursor
7dw	deletes the word following the cursor and six words to the right
dd	deletes the line occupied by the cursor
3dd	deletes the line occupied by the cursor and two lines following
D	deletes from the current cursor position to the end of the line

Three of the commands include numbers (2, 7 or 3). By inserting different numbers, you can delete different number of characters, words or lines.

Undelete

To undo the last delete with the command:

u

To undo all the deletions on a given line use the command:

U

Some simple examples

Moving text

The easiest way to move text is to delete it and then paste it from the default buffer. To restore deleted text use the following:

p	the deleted text is placed after the cursor
P	the deleted text is placed before the cursor

You can use all the commands for deleting, mentioned above. For example, to move five lines from one place to another, complete the following steps:

1. Enter full screen mode by pressing <Esc>.
2. Move the cursor to the first of five lines to be moved.
3. Delete the lines by entering **5dd**.
4. Move the cursor to the line above the desired position.
5. Press **p**.
6. The lines are inserted on the line below the position of the cursor.

Copying text

Use the **yank** command to copy text. **yank** copies text into a buffer (intermediate storage). To move the text, place the cursor at the targeted position and retrieve the text from the buffer using **p** or **P**.

For example, to copy two lines:

1. Make sure you are in full screen mode by pressing <Esc>.
2. Move the cursor to the beginning of the lines to be copied
3. Yank 2 lines to the default buffer by pressing **2y**
4. Move the cursor to the targeted position
5. Insert the lines by pressing **p.**

Searching for text within a file

While in full screen mode, to find a given text string in a file use the slash (/) command. For example, the following command:

/searchword

searches forward in the current file for *searchword*.

To search again for the same text, you can repeat the last search by pressing **n**. To search backwards, use **?** instead of /.

Search and replace

While in command mode, to search for a certain string of text and replace it with another, use the following command:

*%s/oldstring/newstring/***g**

% means search for every occurrence of *oldstring* in the **vi** memory buffer. **s** or substitute substitutes *newstring* for every occurrence of *oldstring*. **g** means global or throughout the file. Without **g** only the first occurrence of *oldstring* is replaced with *newstring*. If you add **c** or:

*%s/oldstring/newstring/***gc**

vi asks you to confirm each change before it is made.

Thus, to replace the word "data" with the word "edp" complete the following steps:

1.   Press <Esc> to make sure you are in full screen mode.
2.   Press <:> to move into command mode.
3.   Enter **%s/data/edp/g**.
4.   Press **<Enter>.**

vi replaces every text string "data" with the text string "edp".

Merging one file into another

To merge or read one file into another, first place the cursor one line above the targeted position. Then use the command:

r *filename*

(or read *filename*) to merge *filename* into the current file.

Using vi keystroke abbreviations (macros)

vi full screen and command mode commands can be abbreviated with **ab** (abbreviate) and **map**. Both allow you to assign (or map) a command or series of commands to one or two keystrokes. Mapping commands can be defined from within a **vi** session while in command mode, or they can be defined globally for every session in your *$HOME/.exrc* file. The following are samples from the author's *.exrc* file, but they can be issued at a colon (**:**) prompt in command mode as well. The following assumes that you are entering the command at the command mode prompt inside a given **vi** session.

ab aa 'a,'b
This abbreviates the **vi** define block keystrokes **'a,'b** to **aa**. (For more information on defining blocks of text, see the section on defining blocks of text above).

map ,d :aa d^M
Assuming you have completed the abbreviation above, this map causes the keystrokes **,d** to **d**elete to buffer **a** the text block marked by **'a,'b**. To include the ^M character you must use **vi**'s **<Ctrl>v** feature. To enter the ^M, type **<Ctrl>v** and press **<Enter>**.

map ,p "ap^M
This map causes the keystrokes **<Ctrl>p** to **p**ut the contents of buffer **a** after the cursor location. To enter the ^M, type **<Ctrl>v** and press **<Enter>**.

map ,m :aa m.^M
Similarly, this map causes the keystrokes **<Ctrl>m** to move the lines defined by **'a,'b** to the line following the cursor location. "move marked lines to cursor location. To enter the ^M, type **<Ctrl>v** and press **<Enter>**.

map ,c :aa co.^M
This map causes the keystrokes **<Ctrl>c** to copy the lines defined by **'a,'b** to the line following the cursor location. To enter the ^M, type **<Ctrl>v** and press **<Enter>**.

Appendix C
System function with DOS and UNIX command equivalents

This table shows system function together with DOS and UNIX command equivalents. While the UNIX command listed below can perform functions equivalent to the listed DOS commands, in many cases the UNIX commands are much more robust than their DOS cousins. Consult the article on the command in question before using the command.

NOTE:
SCO UNIX, Solaris and UnixWare are available with a DOS emulator (e.g., Locus Computing Corporation's Merge 386™). If your version of UNIX is equipped with a DOS emulator, it is often easier and better to use actual DOS or DR.DOS™ commands supplied with the emulator rather than their UNIX equivalents.

System Function	DOS command	UNIX command	Comments
back up files	**backup**	**backup** **mt**	**backup** is used by SCO UNIX and **mt** is used by Solaris to backup UNIX files and filesystems.
change directories	**cd**	**cd**	
check and reports disk status	**chkdsk**	**df** **dfspace**	**df** shows the number of free blocks and inodes in a file system. **dfspace** displays the total disk space (in Mbytes), space available and percentage used.

clear screen	**cls**	**clear**	UNIX can be set to use **cls**. See **ln** or C-shell.
start a command interpreter	**command**	**sh** **csh** **ksh**	**sh** starts a Bourne command shell. **csh** starts a C-shell command shell. **ksh** starts a Korn command shell.
copy files	**copy**	**cp, copy, tar, dd**	**cp** is closest to **copy**. The other commands can be used to perform more complex tasks, e.g., copying whole directories, making disk images to backing up files to tape or disk.
display system date and time	**date**	**date** **cal**	UNIX uses **date** to display or change the system date and time and **cal** to display a three month calendar.
delete a file	**del**	**rm**	**rm** is more powerful than **del**. With **rm**, you can remove directories as well as files.
list the contents of a directory	**dir**	**ls** **lf** **l** **lc**	These all list the contents of a directory. Each presents the information using slightly differing formats.
find text inside a file	**find**	**grep** **egrep** **fgrep**	finds text inside a file. UNIX has a **find** command the finds files in the UNIX file system.
format a disk	**format**	**format**	The UNIX system **format** command formats a disk for use with the UNIX system. To format a DOS disk, use **dosformat**.
creates a directory	**mkdir**	**mkdir**	
prints text files in the background	**print**	**lp** **lpr**	Both commands cause files to be placed in the UNIX print queue. The UNIX print scheduler then directs files to printers.
renames files	**ren**	**mv**	**mv** "moves" a file to a different place or name.

UNIX commands by example

restores files made with the **backup** command	**restore**	**restore**	
removes a directory	**rmdir**	**rmdir** **rm -r**	**rm -r** removes directories that contain files. **rmdir** can only remove empty directories.
sort data	**sort**	**sort**	
display a text file on the screen	**type**	**cat** **more** **pg** **less**	**more, pg** and **less** all display the file contents one screen at a time.
recovers files that have been deleted	**undelete**		UNIX systems use a variety of methods to recover files. See "C-shell Configuring your work environment" for an example using the **alias** command.
copy files and directories	**xcopy**	**copy** **cpio** **tar**	**copy** is closest to **xcopy**. The other commands can be used to perform more complex tasks, e.g., copying complete filesystems to a single file or backing up the files to floppy disk or tape.